UP-CLOSE AND PERSONAL

UP-CLOSE AND PERSONAL
THE RISE OF THE TRUMPLICAN PARTY

LIONEL B. HARRIS

ReadersMagnet, LLC

Up-Close and Personal: The Rise of the Trumplican Party
Copyright © 2020 by Lionel B. Harris

This book is written to provide information and motivation to readers. Its purpose is not to render any type of psychological, legal, or professional advice of any kind. The content is the sole opinion and expression of the author, and not necessarily that of the publisher.

Published in the United States of America
ISBN Paperback: 978-1-952896-29-3
ISBN eBook: 978-1-952896-30-9

All rights reserved. No part of this publication may be reproduced, stored in a retrieval system or transmitted in any way by any means, electronic, mechanical, photocopy, recording or otherwise without the prior permission of the author except as provided by USA copyright law.

Scriptures marked KJV are taken from *King James Version* (KJV): *King James Version*, public domain.

The opinions expressed by the author are not necessarily those of ReadersMagnet, LLC.

ReadersMagnet, LLC
10620 Treena Street, Suite 230 | San Diego, California, 92131 USA
1.619.354.2643 | www.readersmagnet.com

Book design copyright © 2020 by ReadersMagnet, LLC. All rights reserved.
Cover design by Ericka Obando
Interior design by Shemaryl Tampus

This book is written to provide information and a degree of enlightenment to readers. Its purpose is not to render any type of psychological, legal, or professional advice of any kind. Its content is the sole opinion and expression of the author, and not necessarily that of the publisher.

CONTENTS

ABOUT THE AUTHOR ix

PROLOGUE. xi

"DRAINING THE SWAMP". 1

"SAVE ALL THE CHILDREN" 12

"THE SHAME OF IT ALL". .25

"THE ART OF BEING FOOLISH". 37

"THE BULLY BEHIND THE PULPIT". 47

"THE EVIL THAT MEN DO" 62

"IN PURSUIT OF COMPASSION AND EMPATHY". . .73

"CHRISTIANS, EVANGELICALS AND DEVILS" 91

"UP CLOSE AND PERSONAL" 105

"ANATOMY OF AN ORANGE LEMON". 122

EPILOGUE 135

IN LOVING MEMORY OF -

My wife - *GLORIA*
My mother - *RUBY*
My uncle - *BILL*
My brother - *TARAN*
My brother - *GARY*
&
My dear friend -
DORIS JOHNSON

I dearly miss each and
Every one of them and I
Thank God for crossing
Our path!

ABOUT THE AUTHOR

"*LIONEL BARRY HARRIS*" IS A native of the city of Saint Louis, Missouri. After serving a three-year tour in United States Army and obtaining the rank of sergeant E-5, he persistently pursued his writing desires while, simultaneously engaging in a whole gamut of diverse and interesting jobs. Along with managing a large janitorial service in the state of Indiana (at the age of twenty-two), he returned to Missouri and was subsequently employed by the federal government, the Saint Louis Police Department, the Wagner Electric Company, the Potter Electric Company and, the most gratifying and enduring of them all (thirty-four years), the Saint Louis Public Schools at the high school level. In addition to the foregoing, Harris worked part-time in the GED educational program, served as a department store salesman, drove a school bus for the Ferguson-Florissant School District (six years) and, afterwards, drove a courtesy bus for senior citizens in Saint Louis county (three years). Although HARRIS penned "Up-Close and Personal," he also authored "Racism, Sexism, Trumpism, Pseudo-Christianity and the Cinema," "Dark Yesterdays - Bright Tomorrows," "The Long and Winding Road" and "On the Wings of Tragedy."

★ ★ ★

PROLOGUE

In late November of 2019, Rick Perry, who was the Trump administration's former Secretary of Energy, declared that Donald John Trump was the "Chosen One." Without so much as a facial smirk or a wink of an eye, Mr. Perry boldly stated that the sitting POTUS was "divinely" favored by the Supreme Being Himself.

Obviously, I don't know how that assertion resonated with the average American citizen, but, personally, I was taken aback. More than that, I was appalled and deeply anguished by it. To merely suggest that President Trump is, somehow, a "benevolent" instrument of God was totally foreign and incoherent to me. As some people like to say, I could not begin to "wrap my head around" such an absurd and asinine comment.

However, that was my initial reaction and, admittedly, a snap reaction that arose from my longtime familiarity with Donald Trump, the man. Fact is, I'm a seventy-five year old black man (older than the President himself) and I am well-aware of Mr. Trump's lengthy and well-documented track record. And he may or may not be a white supremacist (the jury is still out on that charge) but he's certainly a closet racist, an egotist, a sociopath and a chronic liar. Focusing on just those four personality disorders, I thoroughly believe Donald Trump does not have a religious bone in his entire body!

But that does not mean that the President is a pariah or an outcast in the eyes of God. It certainly doesn't indicate that the Supreme Being has written off Mr. Trump - or any other

PROLOGUE

individual of ill-repute and sinfulness. I've been eyewitness to so many people who subjected themselves to heartfelt repentance and regret and, alternately, turned their lives around. And as long as the Commander-in-Chief lives and breathes, he, too, is susceptible to God's forgiveness and gracious mercy.

Therefore, when I hastily took issue with Rick Perry verbally anointing Trump as the "Chosen One," I was speaking solely from an emotional viewpoint. In a certain sense, I was speaking before I took time to think rationally and without any semblance of prejudgment. That, in itself, is quite difficult.

Even before Rick Perry attempted to exalt and affiliate Donald Trump with God's supreme favor, I had heard other individuals of prominence (all of them, Republicans and Trump surrogates) suggest that the President was "divinely" selected to become America's Chief Executive and while I was dismissive of all of the foregoing assertions, I didn't attach seriousness to the premise until Perry's on-camera opinion was voiced in the waning days of November 2019. After much deliberation, weighing all the pros and cons, I came up with a perspective (or hypothesis) that, in some regards, parallels Rick Perry's pronouncement. Some people might deem it as mere semantics, others may accuse me of "splitting hairs," but words do matter.

Therefore, when I denounce Donald Trump as the "Chosen One" and advocate that he more so be considered the "selected one" instead, I am acknowledging God's sovereign influence in the matter. I am not about to lie and claim that God spoke to me directly, saying that He sanctioned Donald Trump's presidency, but I've never viewed the installment as a mistake or mere happenstance. I truly believe it was God's divine will and I'll venture to tell you why I feel that way.

First and foremost, I am not a religious fanatic. Although I aspire and long to be one, I don't even consider myself a bonafide Christian. I don't regularly attend church services (like I once did), I don't pray (as much as I should) and I no longer donate monies to the less fortunate (like I frequently did in the past).

UP-CLOSE AND PERSONAL

Although the Trump presidency is froth with continuous strife and controversy, I remain optimistic and hopeful. I keep reminding myself (and others) that, "This, too, shall pass." More importantly, and I wish someone of prominence or influence would tell the Republican Party that, "There is life after President Donald Trump."

However, before we can watch our current POTUS ride off into the setting sun (whether with faces of glee or gloom), let us try to remember what the United States of America looked like prior to Trump taking the oath of office in January of 2017. We, as mortal men and women, may need prescription bifocals or even a magnifying glass but God has 20-20 vision. He sees indiscriminately and regardless of a person's race, religion, creed or their station in life.

Naturally, I cannot lay claim to seeing the overall state of America through God's omniscient eyes, neither "prior to" Trump's election or "at present." I am not an Evangelist or a prophet either. Therefore, I do not have the gall to deem my words or opines as gospel. I'm only speculating and inferring, which is mostly predicated on my senior citizen status, my varied life-experiences and, most certainly, my racial identity. And if you (the reader) think I'm being curt or catty, I assure you I'm not. I have long believed that a white person and a black person can simultaneously observe the same evening sunset and come away, describing it as entirely different. So, not only am I unable to see things through God's eyes, I can't see them through Caucasian eyes or any other race's eyes either - and there lies the overwhelming disconnect of the American populous.

In God's infinite wisdom, I truly believe that He, Himself, purposely orchestrated Donald Trump's ascension to the United States presidency. And I believe it wasn't because the Supreme Being disfavored Hillary Clinton, it wasn't due to some degree of divine boredom or frivolity, it wasn't due to a random, free-wheeling experiment and it was not in the name of some kind of blanket punishment mechanism either, one that was especially

PROLOGUE

aimed at faithless or backsliding American citizens (although some individuals might very well perceive it as such).

Notably, I have an entirely different take on God's role in the matter. It is said that God "Works in mysterious ways" and when I reflect on our Lord at great lengths, clearly cognizant that He is the same God we traditionally worship, highly exalt and read about in, both, the Old and the New Testaments, it is more than evident that His "ways" are, oftentimes, totally contrary (and, frequently, confounding as well) to humankind's ways and means.

For instance, He's the same God who implored Egypt's sovereign ruler to "Let my people go!" and, then, hardened Pharaoh's heart, compelling the leader to be resistant to God's beseechment. He's the same Lord who sacrificed His only begotten son, fully aware that that son would suffer agonizing physical and mental pain. In addition, He's the very God who transformed the callous, non-believing Saul into the repentive and prolific Saint Paul. And, in my personal estimation, He is the very same God who installed Barack Obama as America's first African-American president - and was divinely cognizant that Donald J. Trump would soon succeed him.

Again, I reaffirm that the foregoing is my personal hypothesis. And I proudly own it. Admittedly, it's controversial and unprovable also, but I thoroughly believe it was strategically planned, precisely mapped out. For example, if George W. Bush had not been so inept and defective as a POTUS, as well as the chief orchestrator of the unjustified war in Iraq, Caucasian voters (even classic bigots) would not have held their noses and temporarily stifled their racial biasness. In addition, although I'll incur further criticism for saying so, it was a "turn-off" that Hillary Clinton was a woman too. I reemphasize, I do not believe that Mrs. Clinton was remotely disfavored by God; neither when she opposed Obama for the democratic nomination or Trump for the presidency itself, but the Supreme Being was also fully aware of how embedded and pervasive male chauvinism "was" and still "is" in our country.

UP-CLOSE AND PERSONAL

I am positive I'll be further demeaned and criticized for, yet, another homespun analogy too. I'm sure it will raise the dander of many white people and a number of black folks as well. Call me stupid or plain-old ridiculous, but I truly suspected that Barack Obama's electability status was bolstered merely because he was, in fact, biracial as well. That subtle little difference is, often times, a large difference to "closet" and "lukewarm" bigots. That factor, too, garnered uncalculated votes for Obama. Am I advocating that there was a cluster of citizens who voted for the 44th president because he was half-white? Emphatically YES!

Now, if that foregoing assertion strikes you as non-sensible and entirely preposterous, then guess what? You and I are essentially on the same page. However, because I'm adorned with black skin and, maybe, more senior than you (the reader), I might be a couple of paragraphs ahead of you in that hypothetical book. I, therefore, submit to you that there are select individuals in this country (white ones and a number of black ones too) who are more tolerable of biracial citizens. If you brand that absurd, then take a moment and ponder this: Light skin African-Americans (Obama included) are less discriminated against than their darker brothers and sisters. I've always deemed that mindset as absurd and sick but, nevertheless, it's true. It is also irrational and unexplainable. I have locked horns with racism all my life (in civilian life and the military). I staunchly opposed it and called it out.

But I have never, and I emphasize "never" come close to understand racial animus and I am positive I never will. But, tragically, it has tremendous staying power. Racism is deeply entrenched and methodically sewn into America's fabric. Oh, it might subside to a small degree, it may go underground for a brief period also, and it might even attempt to disguise or revamp itself (try to sell itself as "nationalism" or "patriotism"), but it always resurfaces - somewhat like an infestation of rats and roaches.

In the scriptures, Jesus reportedly said, "The poor will always be with us" and I grievously fear the very same applies to racial discrimination. For some bizarre and incomprehensible rationale, people (and not only Caucasians) feel uplifted, superior and emboldened when looking down at individuals who are racially different from them. That, to me, has always been extremely sickening, perverse and blatantly ungodly.

Some folks (probably naive Americans and onlooking foreigners) might have thought racism in the United States was on hiatus in light of Barack Obama's two-term presidency. And some people (even Americans) may have even surmised it was showing signs of dissolving or shrinking when the 44th president took the oath of office - but they could not have been more wrong. Yesteryear black activist, H. Rap Brown, once stated (and I'm paraphrasing) that "Violence in America is as common as cherry pie." And guess what? Racism is even more common. It has never been on holiday and it's not dissipating or waning either. On the contrary, it is seething, intense and clearly on the rise.

I submit to you that God was fully aware of all of the aforementioned commentary and happenings and much, much more - and, notably, well-prior to Donald Trump's presidential run. But I surmise that God was acutely cognizant of something else as well, something even more nefarious and disturbing. God has a discriminate and censuring eye on mankind's duo-headed "gods" also. And history proves that those gods are formidable, highly exalted and ever-present.

Those two gods, who function in extremely close concert, are specifically identified as *"money"* (essentially the relentless pursuit of it) and *"power"* and, sorrowfully, their worship appeal not only rivals that of the living God, it frequently surpasses and trounces it. And that unholy alienation, I truly believe was a major part of the *"whole"* picture God visualized in pre-Trump years and He was moderately disenchanted, but not at all surprised by it. After all, the Supreme Being well-knows that a rather "fickle" mankind is subject to all variations of sinfulness and lawlessness. And that includes avarice, whoremongering, rape, racism, genocide, misogyny, adultery, murder and much more. And since Donald J. Trump could be officially cited as a *"poster boy"* for a number of those unsavory offenses, God pre-selected him as the express focal point for His revealing and comprehensive expose.

However, in doing so, the Supreme Being well knew that Mr. Trump was not a singular enigma, certainly not a man who is void of human commonality. God is keenly aware that, "Birds of a feather flock together." Even though Trump is outrageous, God doesn't deem him unique. Therefore, God knew it was fitting that His all-powerful searchlight be brightly shined upon Trump surrogates and like-minded constituents also. Not so coincidentally, Mr. Trump's close-knit cohorts are devoutly enamored with money and power too.

In reality, God's expose is not exclusively aimed at President Trump and his lock-step cohorts either. Many fellow Americans, even Anti-Trumpers and individuals who long for the end of Trump's presidency, are guilty of exalting and worshipping those exact two pseudo-gods. Inevitably, those people will be held accountable for their alienation and betrayal to the authentic God also. At this precise moment in time, however, it suffices to contend that "money" does not guarantee a person's true happiness and its ally, "power", oftentimes leads to graft and corruption.

The ongoing behavior and actions of the Donald Trump administration loudly cries out for immediate and serious attention, not only the Lord's attention but attention from discerning and faith-based Americans as well. Our sitting POTUS leads and inspires a loyal coalition of unprincipled and self-serving men and women (and Vice-President Pence is certainly amongst them) and Trump and his confederates are inflicting untold harm on our entire country on a daily basis. And so much of that harm has prolong and lingering effects. In my assessment, Donald J. Trump is the ideal prototype for such outrageous and devastating behavior.

In summation, I digress by echoing something I originally stated. "Donald Trump doesn't have a religious bone in his entire

PROLOGUE

body!" And I could square off with Rick Perry all day long, denouncing the President as the "Chosen One" and insisting, instead, that the POTUS is, without a semblance of doubt, a pre-selected instrument of God. And to be even more precise, totally unbeknownst to Mr. Trump himself, he is the lead star of one of God's complex and incomprehensible mysteries. Whether you loathe or adore President Trump, you have to admit the man's a real "piece of work!" And that's not even debatable.

"DRAINING THE SWAMP"

During Donald Trump's presidential campaign against former Secretary of State, Hillary Clinton, Trump felt it was "fair game" to showcase (via television) a number of different women who alleged that former President Bill Clinton was an adulterer, a sexual predator and/or a rapist. That unprecedented move struck me as cruel, hypocritical and totally ludicrous.

Fact was, Hillary's husband was not running for a third presidential term and Mr. Trump, a personified skillet, was calling the kettle "black." Well-known as somewhat of a playboy and a womanizer his self (it was before the Access Hollywood tape surfaced), the "Donald" was not an upstanding, stellar angel. During the succeeding months, all of America learned that when he proudly paraded out Bill Clinton's female accusers, he (as my dear mother used to say) "had more nerve than a brass monkey."

Now, I have no idea how much sustained damage was done to Mrs. Clinton's campaign on behalf of Trump's unorthodox assault on the character of Bill Clinton, Hillary's husband. All I know is it was nonsensible and grossly unfair. If white voters, especially white women, changed their support to Trump even partially in light of Trump's mean-spirited tactic, it says something revealing about them, not only the Republican challenger. It says they were actually against Hillary Clinton all along and they welcomed, yet, another reason to oppose her. The sad reality is this, and I apologize for my bluntness in the matter, although William Jefferson Clinton might have been guilty of "some" or "all" of the charges of marital infidelity that was levelled by his accusers, he was certainly not an enigma. I've been around men all my long life, single men, divorced men and married ones as well, and I have known few of them who remained faithful to their wives, their girlfriends or their boyfriends. And regardless of race or gender, most of their love counterparts know that's true. Many of the respective mates were forgiving when it came to their man's infidelity - so why hold Hillary accountable for Bill's unfaithfulness? Hopefully, your love partner is an exception to my narrative.

Well before Donald Trump tossed his hat into the presidential ring, he had a marked and almost insane hatred for President Barack Obama. He arrogantly owned it and actively promoted the so-called "birther movement," which falsely claimed that this country's first African-American president was not born in the United States. However, well before Mr. Trump attempted to delegitimize Obama's two-term presidency, he was renowned for his rather blood-thirsty behavior, both, 'during' and 'after' the "Central Park Five" fiasco. In that well-publicized case, although the accused black suspects were, alternately, cleared and exonerated for the alleged crimes, Donald Trump was practically obsessed with having them punished and incarcerated none the less. And, to me, it's the real Donald John Trump in real time.

Therefore, many decades before America's President called African-American football players "sons-of-bitches," before he openly disparaged predominantly-black inner cities such as Chicago, Illinois and Baltimore, Maryland, before he boisterously labelled poverty *stricken* and war torn African (and dark-skinned) nations "Shit-hole countries," and even prior to his vacillating and lukewarm denouncement of Neo-Nazi and white supremacy factions in Charlottesville, Virginia, Mr. Trump was already an aspiring and vindictive racist. And, from my perspective, I thoroughly believe he reached his supreme goal many, many years ago.

Furthermore, from my personal standpoint as well, when Trump became POTUS and audaciously announced, "I am the least racist person you know," he was not only lying through his teeth (something he does to sheer perfection), he added to his 'questionable' resume. He instantly became a comical racist.

His assertion, however, sparked a sorrowful memory in me. It caused me to vividly recall Governor George Wallace, who, prior to launching his own presidential campaign in the nineteen sixties, stood at the door of the University of Alabama and prevented Negro students from entering. Notably, he's the man who declared, "Segregation today, segregation tomorrow and segregation forever," a slogan which, subsequently, rendered him somewhat comical also.

In 2017, when an American soldier lost his life in military action in Niger, Africa, President Donald Trump struggled with a weighty dilemma (at least, to him). Since he was also the Commander-in-Chief, he was dutifully faced with the solemn task of telephoning the fallen soldier's widow and offering her his sincere condolences.

However, since Sgt. LaDavid Johnson happened to be an African-American, Trump felt somewhat ill at-ease when he was slated to dialogue with the sergeant's grieving widow and family. Eventually, the President did make the call - but not before he consulted his, then, Chief-of-Staff, John Kelly. Because the POTUS was well-aware that General Kelly had lost a son in military action, Trump was in search of some degree of insight.

At first thought, one would assume that it was a rational and innocent idea. Seeking advice from an individual who knew what it was like to lose a loved one to military warfare, and especially since the advisor was a retired general, was quite commendable. However, when the President, subsequently, did converse with Mrs. Johnson and decided to remind her that her deceased husband "signed up for it" (meaning the sergeant volunteered for active duty), John Kelly's beforehand counsel fell somewhat short. I don't know about other people, but that particular footnote would not be a comfort to me. And solely because Sgt. Johnson was,

"DRAINING THE SWAMP"

indeed, black, focusing on Trump's unsavory past, his lament fell considerably short also.

I am more than positive that some people would chide me, and especially Caucasian people. They would strongly accuse me of being grossly biased when it comes to Donald Trump. They might even brand me a hate-monger or a black bigot (or the other slur). And they'd be correct about the "bias" charge, but not the latter one. As I pointed out, my disdain for the man is anchored in his past history. It's not because he's white, or because he's wealthy, and it's not even because he's a serial liar. Almost exclusively, it is about the President's despicable character. Over the years, I've been convinced he is completely void of compassion, empathy and heartfelt sympathy. And, alarmingly, that's just the tip of the iceberg.

However, the LaDavid Johnson incident is not the sole basis for my feelings. Certainly, Sgt. Johnson was an African-American but skin color and migrant origin are not the overwhelming basis for the President's lack of authentic compassion. In a certain sense, he's an equal-opportunity offender.

Before Senator John McCain passed away (of terminal cancer), the Senator made it clear that he did not want President Trump to attend his eminent funeral. The request was unprecedented but, while many people concluded that the Senator hated Trump, I surmised that McCain saw the man as I see him. The POTUS frequently uses the word "fake" and the Senator wanted no parts of Trump's fake or feigned compassion and, therefore, did not wish to provide Mr. Trump a photo-opportunity.

After all, the President had made a series of derogatory remarks about Senator McCain, who was a celebrated war hero and a former P.O.W. And among those remarks, or digs, was "My heroes don't get captured" and for a suspect draft-dodger who didn't know a low-quarter shoe from a combat boot (my dig), Trump should have remained entirely mum. In addition, since the Senator was acutely aware that Trump solely blamed him for preventing the repeal of "Obama Care," McCain was fully aware of the man's intense distaste for him.

Of course, Trump, being the vindictive and begrudging individual we've come to know, did not permit his insensitivity and callousness to die with John McCain. Instead, he chose to focus on the Senator's grieving family and loved ones and kept the insults fresh and ever-present. And that particular behavior, sadly, typifies our sitting President.

Frankly speaking, I well-know that my personal empathy and sympathy works overtime. Every day (owing to cable and network TV), I fight depression in the wake of viewing the devastating and horrific happenings that continually plague our country and its populace. And whether the victimized people are black, white, yellow, red or brown, my heart virtually agonizes for their diverse plights. In realizing that "they," any one of them, could be me or someone I dearly love and cherish, keeps me humbled and well-grounded.

Therefore, towards the end of 2019, when it was revealed that Donald Trump had taken nefarious steps to bring, both, Joe and Hunter Biden into his warped and seedy orbit, my heart was filled with sorrow and anguish. My immediate thoughts were: Here is a man, meaning Joe Biden, a man who was the former Vice-President of the United States, and a person who had already suffered his share of life's random hardships - and now he has to reckon with the callousness and devious actions of a Donald Trump.

Years ago, Joe Biden lost a wife and 'a daughter in a terrible automobile accident and, just a few years back, mourned the loss of, yet, another son to cancer. But not at all surprising, none of the foregoing tragedies remotely restrained or touched the heart of Donald Trump. In actuality, purposefully embroidering Hunter Biden, Joe Biden's remaining son, in political controversy and unproven charges of corruption and graft is right out of the Trump playbook. It apparently advocates taking no prisoners, running completely roughshod of common decency and doing irreparable harm to children, if they benefit your shady schemes. In essence, anything and everything are on Trump's political table, regardless of who is, alternately, injured or destroyed.

Charge me with being melodramatic, if you wish, but I can't help but wonder how a Donald Trump might have fared if he had been made to walk in Joseph Biden's shoes. Although our "silver spoon" POTUS may think he's entirely immune to unforeseen tragedies, he is grossly in error. Sudden or inevitable death could have reached out and touched any one of Trump's loved ones and neither money nor great power could have exempted them from it. I do not wish any of them ill-will but I can't avoid wondering if the President had been subjected to the mournful woes of Joe Biden, would it have, somehow, enhanced the man's lowly character? I seriously doubt it, but it's something to mull over.

When Donald Trump arrogantly claimed he "knew more than the (military) generals," I instantly laughed. When Donald Trump stated he was "a stable genius," I shook my head in sheer awe, in respect to both words.

When Donald Trump closely aligned himself with two foreign dictators (Vladimir Putin and Kim Jong Un), I was practically mortified. But when Donald Trump directed, or ordered, the assorted military branches to stage him a gala "vanity" parade in Washington D.C. (which was undeserved), I was beside myself with disgust.

For a man who, apparently, felt he was above serving in the military (bone spurs, unsubstantiated), I deemed it totally absurd, ludicrous and grossly unfair to America's soldiers, marines, airmen, sailors and etc. I keenly recalled the extensive laboring and rigorist toil that traditionally prevailed when armed forces members readied themselves (under the close scrutiny of their superiors) for an elaborate and comprehensive inspection or any comparable review. In my day, the military brass thought nothing of working soldiers for twenty hours, allowing them to rest for two or three hours, and resuming the cleaning process for another lengthy period. All for the sake of a General-headed inspection process that may have lasted well-short of two hours. Therefore, I greatly dreaded what active duty personnel endured while being made to prepare for a lavish, staged and unprecedented parade in our national capitol.

My personal reminiscence, although dated, was not unique or farfetched however. I've interacted with a number of veterans who served many years after I did and, not at all surprising, their military experiences were similar to mine. Comparable drills, same rigid training, same old complaints ("Hurry up and wait"), same regimental and repetitious cleaning routines and even periods of sleep-deprivation. But, I'll venture to surmise, none of us were hit with a surprise, unwarranted parade, and especially one that required a ton of money, massive troop movements, air-lifts and, most disturbing (to the involved troops), the unsuspected high-jacking of a traditional, national holiday. And I imagine that was a factor that affected the military enlistees and their respective families.

Admittedly, my personalized contempt for President Trump and his self-adoration parade (not to dismiss his phony deferment) goes much deeper than my heartfelt empathy for active duty service people. I acutely, and painfully, remember how things were when I wore an army uniform and, believe me, it was not a picnic in the park.

I served in the United States army from June of 1962 until June of 1965 and was, eventually, discharged as a Sgt. E-5. When I enlisted, I was paid the menial salary of $78.00 a month and, still, I took the initiative to send $40.00 of it home. With the government tossing in an additional forty dollars, it was called an "allotment." Although I volunteered for South Vietnam at one point (but was denied), the only war I fought was the war against racial discrimination and it was a formidable foe.

As I priory disclosed, I am a black man, a rather proud black man and I was even proud to verbally cite, both, John F. Kennedy and Lyndon B. Johnson as my respective Commanders-In-Chief when I served in the military. The racial biasness and turmoil I encountered came from individuals who were on the lower tiers of the Chain of Command (such as sergeants and low-levelled officers) and, therefore, I cannot justly fault either of the foretasted Chief Executives for the problems I incurred during my soldiering stint. However, I wasn't alone in my combat against racism. It was commonplace and widespread in those days.

However, in spite of vividly recalling those bygone days, and some of them were downright frustrating, I thank the living God for a single, select favor. I'm sincerely grateful for not serving under a Commander-In-Chief who was like a Donald John Trump. For, to me, the man's a total vexation to my spirit and a complete embarrassment as a President.

In retrospect, Trump is not the only POTUS who didn't serve in the armed forces and he's not the only Chief Executive who abused and usurped his powers either (Richard M. Nixon comes to mind). But, in my estimation, he's "a clear and present danger" and instead of getting better, he worsens every day. I view Trump as a lone, unhinged maverick, and one who sincerely believes he knows everything about anything. And that brinks on sheer insanity.

As you see, I make no bones for my opposition towards Donald Trump. But, as a former active duty soldier who is now an elderly, seasoned veteran, I can't help from wondering how the current crop of American fighting men and women feel about him. I mean, honestly feel about him! Oh, I know he pays them well. He's even poised to give service people a substantial raise in 2020. But while the POTUS thinks it is, money is not everything.

In the core of their hearts, what do soldiers actually think of a man who feels he's too valuable and elitist to serve in the military? A Commander-In-Chief who views American troops as "mercenaries" and even worse, "killing machines?" How do soldiers (regardless of gender) feel about a President who would lease their services out to the highest bidder, to foreign countries such as Saudi Arabia? And, furthermore, what do combat troop's think of a man who would prefer to see them dead than see them taken prisoner?

I don't know, I do realize that many individuals think that money is everything. As I stated, Trump believes it wholeheartedly and covets it. He also believes he can give tax breaks to civilians and well publicized raises to the military and they'll, alternately and forever, keep him in their good graces, which translates into Trumpian support and votes at the polls. The POTUS feels he is owed that allegiance.

But the brilliant, would-be general (Trump, of course) views the military as part of his loyal base but, sometimes, he recklessly slips up. He doesn't want to get on the bad side of the military apparatus. And that's what he managed to do when he poked his nose into the "Chief Edward Gallagher" affair in late 2019. Totally ignorant to "esprit de corps," which is a code of comradeship for soldiers, Trump acted foolhardy when he took steps to exonerate and reverse the Navy seal's demotion penalty and blatantly slapped the faces of Gallagher's team accusers and critics. It was an ill-advised decision and one that led to Secretary Richard Spencer's resignation in protest. Then, the fall-out heat set in (from the military brass, outraged politicians and fellow soldiers), Donald Trump got jittery, and he had to remove himself from the hot kitchen. So where did he elect to go? It happened to be Thanksgiving, so he made a surprise visit to Afghanistan for a strategic "photo op."

At that juncture, people could say, "What a wonderful, gracious and brave President he is. He went to a war-zone on behalf of his dedicated love for the troops."

Poppycock! The man went there for distraction from the Eddie Gallagher misstep and the shoring up of votes for the 2020 election. Like a sleight of hand artist, the POTUS considers himself a master of deception. That's why he tells his base (and

"DRAINING THE SWAMP"

they eat it up with a tablespoon) not to believe what they see or what they hear - just believe him. He feeds daily on their overt gullibility and ignorance. Therefore, when he claimed he "knew more than the generals," they were his select and target audience.

Admittedly, I pulled no punches during my heartrending effort to convey how I personally view and feel about President Donald Trump. I see him as a charismatic, but extremely polarizing figure. Not only is he a racist and a nationalist, he's a sociopath, an egotist, a sexual predator, a closet misogynist, a notorious liar and an atheist-in-secret and, therefore, he's an individual who is void of scruples or a moral code of honor. And, to me, he's nothing short of being a social pariah.

However, I must give the man his just due. Although I still take issue with his "stable genius" claim, I thoroughly believe he has great insight. Well-before Trump started his presidential run, he was acutely aware of the underlying (or underground) current in this country. Specifically, he knew just how pervasive, heartfelt and well-entrenched racism and anti-Semitism was in the United States. In addition, since he had and "has" zero interest in the living God or faith in general, he saw Christianity as farcical and totally fake but was certain he could make political hay with that venue as well. With that being said, Trump was cognizant from day-one that an enormous "built-in" base was eagerly awaiting him.

However, Trump's foreseeing (or insight) did not end there, not by a long shot. He peered deeper into his political crystal ball and saw, to his utter delight, the now renown but infamous "swamp." Then, he focused even further and there, in that very swamp, stood (or lurked) individuals who, like him, were enamored with money and power.

Some of the residers he knew and some he didn't, but there stood Steve Bannon, Mick Mulvaney, Michael Cohen, William Barr, Ben Carson, Stephen Miller, Mitch McConnell, John Bolton, Lindsey Graham, John Kennedy (definitely not the beloved President), Sean Spicer, Jeff Sessions, Kellyanne Conway,

UP-CLOSE AND PERSONAL

Rudy Guiliani, Jim Jordan and even Kanye West. And when Trump's lens focused exclusively on Senator McConnell, a man whom he long-esteemed for vowing to make Barack Obama a one-term President, he realized he was home-sweet-home.

So, my question is this: Why, on earth, would the supreme ruler of the so-called "swamp" (Mr. Trump himself, of course) desire to drain it? Why would the Swamp King wish to damage or destroy the site of his "work-pool," from which he frequently extracts his colluding and lock-step henchmen? Therefore, when the POTUS brags about "draining the swamp," it's just another one of his many lies. The hypothetical swamp remains intact, its vile creatures are plentiful and they zealously answer Trump's beckoning calls. Once again, I say, "Birds of a feather flock together."

"SAVE ALL THE CHILDREN"

"When I was a child, I spoke as an adult, I understood as an adult, I thought as an adult, but when I became a grown man, I persistently and joyously pursued my deficient and lost childhood."

Admittedly, that is not how that renowned biblical verse actually reads! You know the one that frequently used the word "*spake*." Contrary to the prose written in 1 Corinthians, Chapter 13, it does not invoke fond memories of a normal or traditional childhood (if there, in fact, is such a thing). Instead, it alludes to a degree of lament and regret. Moreover, it is my personal assessment of my long-ago childhood.

At the ripe old age of 75, I am, indeed, the man-child I referenced in that opening quotation. Of course, I am not claiming that I emerged from my mother's womb, thinking and behaving like a mature adult but it does infer that my preadolescence mindset was considerably different from the greater majority of children I interacted with.

It certainly was not a conscious decision on my part, not some inborn craving to rise above or, in any way, devalue or belittle the worth of the many children around me. Contrarily, I was, seemingly, born with an almost insatiable affection for children, virtually all children, and especially regarding my four biological brothers whom I resided with. In a true sense, it was that irrepressible love feature which was an almost immediate outgrowth from my fractured and troubled childhood. In essence, it was a defense mechanism that was well formulated - even before my wounded childhood limped away into a glistening sunset, never to be seen again.

Had I been an only child, things might have been different. But since I was the second son born in a line-up of five sons (but no sisters), our existence was probably comparable to many ghetto-dwelling Negroid families in those days. Meaning, we had our share of mice, roaches and rats as well. We were relatively poor but (no big deal), I didn't know many black families who weren't poor.

However, there was one thing those poverty-stricken households didn't have. At least, I sincerely hoped they didn't have it. They didn't have a father like the one me and my brothers had. And, also hopefully, their mother didn't have a husband like our mom had either. But as odd as it might sound, I withdrew a measure of comfort from believing that our home circumstances were unique and not at all commonplace.

While my mother was an attractive, petite and light-skinned Negroid woman, my father was considered to be downright handsome (not only in my eyesight and the greater majority of the people who lived around us, but by him - himself). In his conceit, he even verbally described himself as a "pretty man." And upon looking back, I thoroughly believe it was that particular factor, in itself, that severely marred (if not, devastated) his impending life.

Similar to so many so-called "good looking," heterosexual men I've known (yesteryears and today too), my dad thought of himself as "God's gift to women" and he acted accordingly. Sometimes, outward beauty is a curse.

Although I didn't understand my mother's reasoning at the time, my dad's womanizing and ongoing infidelity went basically unchecked. After all, she was a simple country girl who, upon falling in love and, then, being impregnated by a vain and streetwise city-slicker, married him and set up house, just hoping for the best.

Mom seemed to take Dad's sleeping around in stride. I don't recall her nagging him, confronting him or even complaining about him frequently coming home in the wee hours of the night. (Years later, she would contend that, "All men play around and as long as a husband brings his paycheck home, everything was, somewhat, copacetic).

However, even at eight years old I didn't really buy into that rationale. To me, it was totally unfair, it wasn't very nice and it was plain-old sickening. Plus, I always felt what was good for the gander was good for the goose. As I mentioned, my mother was attractive and she didn't dally with men outside her marriage.

But, strangely enough, I became somewhat complicit in my dad's unfaithfulness. When I was that same aforementioned eight year old kid (owing to my small bicycle), I would seek out my father at his favorite two taverns, observe him kissing and/or cuddled up with some very-receptive female and "politely" ask him for a quarter or, sometimes, fifty cents. However, I didn't deem my actions as complicit or "extortion" until much later in my life. In addition to that, I didn't tell my mom or any of my brothers about my spying missions either. (Actually, I was around thirty-two years old when I happened to mention it to my mother).

It is popularly said that, "Give some people an inch and they'll, eventually, take a mile." And that particular saying described my father to a virtual tee. In spite of my mom's penchant for turning a blind eye to my old man's flagrant womanizing, her husband never opted to quit or remotely slow down. If anything, he upped his game by spending select nights away from home altogether.

If marital infidelity stood alone as my father's only vice, I deemed it grossly wrong but I would have softly applauded it. Sorrowfully, that was not the case. In reality, he was anti-God (something I never came to understand), he was a notorious liar, a functional alcoholic (he worked assorted jobs) and, worst of all, he had no qualms against physically or mentally abusing his wife and his stair-step sons, including me. When I was but nine years old, I vividly recall him beating me into a state of semi-unconsciousness

- all because I dared to call him a "liar," which he was. And till this very day, I never regretted my defiance or gall for telling him so.

To be honest, my defiance didn't stop there. Behaving like the tyrant and bully whom he was, my father was virtually fanatical against children dragging their feet. And that was why, in fear of getting a so-called "whipping," my brothers marched around the house like German soldiers. I, on the other hand, purposely dragged my feet and wasn't particularly fearful of his wrath. He could beat me if he wished (and he did for a brief period), but I was poised to die before I knuckled under to him. After a while, he elected to let me alone and find solace from labelling me "crazy." That did not bother me in the least.

Frankly speaking, there was a time when I actually dreamed of "killing" my own father. I'm not proud of that stark admission but when I found myself focusing on my mom's various facial bruises; her bloody noses, her busted lips and blackened eyes, I was adamant about it.

For little or no credible reason at all, my dad would come home and, clearly intoxicated, commence to viciously attack our mother. And regardless of who was present during those occasions; me, my brothers, my maternal grandmother or even a visiting neighbor, he showed no shame, no restraint or mercy and that's what drove me to that dark place during that tumultuous period.

With all of the foregoing said, however, I will now throw you (the reader) somewhat of a curve ball. In the midst of all my father's ongoing womanizing and frequent brutality in our home environment, I constantly worried about him, quietly envied him and, above all, deeply loved the man.

Unfortunately (and to his personal detriment), my dad's aggressive nature did not stop at our home's front stoop and neither did his sporadic recklessness. For instance, one day my oldest brother and I was ordered to trail him up the street where he, alternately, challenged a neighborhood man to a fistfight and was soundly and bloodily defeated. (Secretly, I was glad about

"SAVE ALL THE CHILDREN"

the outcome and was hopeful it had taught my father a lesson in self-restraint).

Then, during, yet, another isolated incident, my father, who was armed with a rather large butcher knife, chased a visiting male neighbor (who was actually twenty years Dad's senior) around and around our living complex but, thankfully, could not catch the man. (Again, I was silently delighted and especially since my father's would-be victim had priorly elected to scold Dad for his unprovoked attack on my mom).

However, in spite of everything; my old man's fooling around, his sporadic and indiscriminate brutality, his in-house tyranny and even his penchant for lying and overall deceitfulness, I still loved and envied him. As to why, I came to believe that only a qualified psychiatrist could have made an educated "guess."

Some people, I imagine, might surmise that I loved my dad merely because he was, indeed, my "father." That, to me, is totally ludicrous and nonsensible. Just because a man (or a woman) is biologically responsible for bringing a child into the world, does not guarantee or justify the respective "seed donors" automatic love and devotion. Tragically, there are some offspring's born into this world who lament their mere existence and silently wish that they had not been born.

Despite my father's exterior beauty, I always wondered if my dad was one of those disgruntled and regretful individuals. What was he really angry about? What made him physically lash out at people who were around him, even individuals who attempted to love him? And, furthermore, why was he so miffed and disenchanted with God? All of those questions persistently clouded my young mind but I was void of any credible answers. Respectfully, I could not bring myself to shun or criticize him. However, it wasn't because I felt he could not present a compelling or adequate argument, it was, more so, due to the underlying envy and admiration I felt towards him.

In my assessment, Dad was strikingly handsome, he had an

attractive, faithful and hard-working wife (Mom worked at a large hospital), he had a steady job (he was a public service bus driver) and, to my utter joy and envy, he fathered five healthy and, relatively, good-looking sons. Therefore, in my opinion, he was genuinely blessed and fortunate. And as strange as it might sound, partially because my father was so unmoved and inappreciative of all of it, I overtly offered him my sincere love and prayed he would someday come to realize his folly and gross errors. But to my heavy sorrow, he never did.

Upon looking back at my troubled childhood and beyond, I viewed myself as, somewhat, of a circus clown. I was endowed with a great sense of humor and had a real knack for making people laugh. That was something me and my quartet of brothers inherited from our mother.

Even when Mom was stressed out (which was much too often), she would always retreat to something amusing and manage to make others around her chuckle and see the bright side of almost every problem. I truly regarded it as God's special gift to my mother and was awfully thankful that it was a transferable personality trait.

However, my mother, just like me, hid discreetly behind that clown's mask and it was downright uncanny how much she and I had in common, and especially when we were made to contend with my volatile father.

While I cannot speak for any of my brothers (of course, they, too, suffered a degree of physical and mental trauma), I was a master at smiling on the outside and crying on the inside. Mirroring my mom, I was always fretful and anguished. But not on my behalf. I was deeply worried - mostly about Mom, my four brothers and, surprising, about my dad too. And, beyond a doubt, he was the main source of all of the ongoing conflict and turmoil.

Although my mother and I did not take out time to compare (until later on in life), there was one thought-pattern that placed us on the same page. Solely because the old man had no qualms or restraint about brawling and raising pure cain (within or outside our residence), we both worried about his physical well-being, and especially when he stayed out extremely late or decided not to come home at all.

Notably, we didn't have a telephone and, therefore, Dad could not call home (even if he was so inclined to do so) and we certainly couldn't call out (even if we had some inkling of where he happened to be).

So, we stayed home and silent, too, my mother and I, practically consumed by fretfulness and quietly imagining that we might be informed of bad or foreboding news regarding Dad at any given moment. Even as we laid awake in our respective beds at night, Mom and I were fearful of a policeman's knock at our front door.

As it came to pass, my father always managed to finally find his way home but, more often than not, he was pissy drunk and filled with hell and brutal rage during those times. Therefore, I'm almost positive that my mother, just like me, came to wish that Dad has stayed put where he previously was. At that point, our collective worriment had instantly dissipated and was, then, replaced by pure dread.

Every now and then my mother would say, "Enough is enough and too much stinks," and when my father's home aggression subsided and then ceased altogether, I could not avoid recollecting that adage.

However, the old man's abrupt change of habit could not be attributed to some miraculous epiphany or Dad's sudden decision to repent and seek God's favor either. (Now, that would have been somewhat of a miracle). Instead, it came about due to two very diverse factors.

Firstly, my father spent days and days away from the home front and, after a while, my mom and I, both, withdrew a measure of relief from his absences. And, secondly (and certainly foremost), my mother came up with a thirty-eight caliber pistol and fiercely ordered him to vacate the house, vowing she'd kill him if he ever again brutalized her or any of her kids.

Periodically, Dad came back home after that episode but never again did he revert back to his old self. Although I was on needles and pins when he was around, I felt somewhat emboldened in knowing where my Mom had hid the gun. I figured if my father's old self happened to show up and my mother could not get to the pistol, I could - and I often day-dreamed about shooting him with it.

No child should be made to entertain such vile and harsh thoughts and no son or daughter should remotely contemplate wounding or killing their father or mother either. Even in my anger and sorrow, I knew it was wrong to host such thoughts. But something had to give. At nine years old, I was at my wits end.

Just in the knick of time, something did give. Prior to turning age ten, my father was completely out of my life (of course that was a revelation that applied to my four brothers and my mother also) and my entire family was in a state of major transition as well. My parent's marriage was officially over (to me, though I occasionally wept, that was a good thing) and since we were void of monetary assistance from my estranged father, we could no longer afford to pay the rent regarding our long-time residence.

My mom, always the optimist, was fond of, yet, another well-known adage. When I was feeling "down and out" (which was far too often for any kid), she would try to pep up my spirits by stating, "When God closes one door, He opens up another door." One day I amusingly tripped her up, responding, "But we don't have a pot to pee in or a window to throw it out - so we don't have no doors."

Thankfully, my mother proved to be right. Just as Mom was at "her" wits end, facing eviction from our long-time residence and quite worried and uncertain as to what to do, her brother-in-law, Bill, came to our rescue. Although there was subdued joy attached to his actions at that time, our Uncle Bill stepped forward and offered my family lodging facilities in his newly-purchased, three-storied house.

Ordinarily, a measure of rejoicement would have prevailed. However, there was a rather sad component to my uncle's gracious offer and it weighed heavily on the hearts and minds of everyone who resided in our large and spacious domicile. Specifically, my mother's elder sister, Hannah, who was Uncle Bill's longtime wife, had recently passed away in that very house. And upon leaving behind her five offspring (our first cousins), she left behind a mournful and somber hole that could not easily be filled. For a lengthy time period, my five cousins (three boys and two girls) were almost inconsolable. Therefore, initially we did not live in a very happy environment, but we made due just the same.

But, on the bright side, my father was no longer in the picture. Not because he had passed away, but, essentially, because he elected to "skip" town, preferring not to pay the court-ordered child support that was imposed on him. To be honest, I had no idea how any of my brothers felt about the old man's sudden departure or his monetary neglect either, but I deeply begrudged him. Notably, it wasn't so much in regards to the money issue (I couldn't begin to imagine how much he faced, having to pay for five kids), but my anger was due to his immediate whereabouts. Since I was aware he had fled to Chicago, Illinois (which was less than four hundred miles away), I blamed him for disappearing entirely and, seemingly, never looking back. And as time marched forward, he became symbolically dead to me.

Although I sincerely mourned my Aunt Hannah's sudden death (I even accompanied my mom to her funeral services), I found myself reflecting on one of my mother's previously mentioned adages. It was the one about God opening up "alternative" doors when life circumstances spiraled dramatically downward. And when my mom was wrestling with serious financial woes, including an impending eviction, it appeared my family's lot could not have gotten much worse.

But, seemingly (although I was never certain that my aunt's coinciding demise had anything to do with it), God stepped forward and changed our fate. Not only did our uncle provide us with a place to live, he and his eldest daughter (who was a private duty nurse) helped my mom financially too. Sitting on the sidelines, that was the "alternative" door I perceived and I was truly appreciative of it.

Although all of my five cousins were older than me, I loved and cherished them even before we formed a somewhat unorthodox nuclear family. With my mother serving as a stand-in matriarch and my uncle representing a surrogate father, two sets of sibling's cohabitating under one large roof, the arrangement worked, and almost to perfection.

My four brothers were pretty closed-mouthed regarding most issues. Therefore, I was unable to gauge how any of them assessed our unusual living circumstances. In my case, however, I applauded it. It wasn't always peaches and cream but it was a far cry better than from "whence" we came.

Still, I was totally unaware of any of my brother's innermost feelings regarding our situation. Naturally, all five of us had different personalities, different emotions and different agendas too.

But when I took time to mull over the circumstances at great lengths, the collective well-being of my siblings was utmost on my young mind. In my heart, I honestly felt our mother would weather any storm (as I stated, she was an eternal optimist) but I was cautiously uncertain about my brothers. Although the passing of time would eventually heal the physical wounds caused by our old man's former aggression, the emotional scars festered and remained untreated. Of course, that was my personal assessment, not that of any of my brothers. However, I was quite sure that each of them could acutely relate to it.

It is said that, "Every dark cloud has a silver lining." I don't know if that's, indeed, true but I certainly hope so. All I know is the following: When it came to my father's exit from my life, I was soon allotted a real-life saving grace. No matter what my brothers or anyone else might have thought, my Uncle Bill emerged as a knight in shining armor to me.

My biological dad and my accommodating uncle (who was not blood-related to me) were as different as night and day. The contrast was downright remarkable!

While my father was considered to be strikingly handsome (and conceited as well), my uncle wasn't deemed attractive in the looks department. In fact, Uncle Bill sported a rather elongated head and was noticeably cock-eyed too. He was a tall, muscular and imposing figure of a man but, inwardly, was soft-spoken, honest and was never quick to anger. And, totally unlike my dad, who could spew out profanity with rapid precision, Uncle Bill never cursed (or cussed) and al-ways kept his cool. Being around my uncle (which I enjoyed), I soon found myself uttering such innocuous words like "dang," "darn," "*boogiejoogie*" and "hot-ta-mighty," words and phrases that kept my mouth out of the gutter and, occasionally, tickled the funny bones of many of my running buddies.

However, the foregoing was not the full extent of what distinguished my uncle from my father. Uncle Bill had a work ethic that I long tried to emulate, but, alternately, put me to shame. Well before his wife died (Aunt Hannah was a stay-at-home wife and mother), Uncle Bill worked eight hours a day on a moving van, came home and ate supper and, then, tackled the evening shift at a local steel foundry. And even as a child, I marveled at his stamina and his perseverance.

Last, but definitely not least, the living God was in the mix also. While Dad could, sadly, be classified as anti-God, my uncle, on the other hand, was pro-God and God-fearing. Even when he appeared to be "dog-tired," Uncle Bill regularly attended church services on Sundays and seemed to enjoy it to the very hilt. In my viewpoint, he showed me what a true Christian looked like and how such a person would behave.

UP-CLOSE AND PERSONAL

In my fondest estimation, my Uncle Bill was a role-model extraordinaire and I've spent a lifetime trying to honor his memory and follow his example. And I've always thanked God for installing him, along with my mother, into my life. And I never took that two-fold blessing for granted because, in reality, it did not have to come to pass.

However, there was something else I never took for granted or overlooked also. Uncle Bill was not perfect (no human being is) and there were two areas in which we greatly disagreed. Invariably, my uncle only saw black or either white. Not race-wise, however. To my uncle, a person (no matter who they were) was either right or was wrong. Again, no exception. But even at ten years old, I often saw shades of gray. And I came to believe that very seldom is a person all wrong or all right. Every issue was based on perception, I came to maintain, and I still feel that way today.

The other area of quiet contention between me and my uncle (actually, we never debated it), in a certain way, had much to do with my M.I.A. father. Uncle Bill was "old-school" in some instances, meaning he shared a particular philosophy that was voiced by a number of elderly men I dealt with in those days. An inordinate number of men, and especially black men, believed it was "unmanly" or "*sissified*" to embrace or kiss male children or any other male for that matter. "Boys and men should only shake hands," they would emphasize, but I never, ever bought into that macho rule.

I've always perceived myself as somewhat of a "serial hugger." No matter if a little girl, a little boy or even a grown man or woman is involved, I have no qualms about reaching out and firmly embracing them. And unless they (the female or male "*huggie*") recoil or opt to spurn my overt affection, they can expect my usual actions time and time again.

As I confessed a while back, I've always had an insatiable love for people (regardless of age, sex, religion or social status) and I make no apologies or excuses for my feelings. And I've also long believed that you give due credit to individuals when they justly deserve it also. My biological father, in spite of all of his vices and flaws, is almost singularly responsible for my affectionate spirit and demonstrative behavior.

For reasons of her own, my mother was seldomly "touchy-feely." She would hug us (her sons) when we were "going to" or "coming back" from a trip or something relevant to those actions, but that was about it. Although she would go to the very max for people she loved (and they were numerous), she never went emotionally overboard. Obviously, that was my mother's way and I never questioned her about it.

However, my father was a different breed. When he wasn't beating up on one of us (his sons), he was not above tightly embracing you or even kissing you on the lips occasionally. And, sometimes, for reasons he failed to divulge, he would even become tearful.

Therefore, when I seriously take the time to look back at my long life, even as I graciously exalt my Uncle Bill as my supreme role-model, I'm obliged to recognize my father as the source of my sensitive side. I truly believe it's a hereditary trait and I'm eternally thankful it was passed down to me.

"THE SHAME OF IT ALL"

As I previously mentioned, I was never the optimist my beloved mother was. And, admittedly, I was never faith-driven like she and my Uncle Bill were either. My traumatic childhood had made me skeptical and a perennial worrier. After so many years of being exposed to my father's volatile conduct when he was still in my life, I could not refrain from being anxious regarding the fate of my residual family.

I worried mostly about my brothers, their mental and physical well-being. I fretted about our immediate future, our financial status and, especially, about my mom's overall health. On the surface she seemed physically fit and sound but a particular thought tormented me. Since death had claimed the lives of four of my mother's biological siblings in less than five years (two sisters and two brothers), I was frequently concerned with her mortality. (To put things into perspective, I always insisted upon accompanying my mom to funerals and, maybe, I was preoccupied with death in general).

I was certain that I would have been personally devastated if Mom abruptly passed away (and so would my four brothers), but a certain question was ever-present on my young mind. If our mother did die, what would become of us, her sons? We'd be, alternately, separated because no one (in their right mind) would take us all in, and intact. As I confessed above, during my childhood, faith was never one of my strong suits.

However, thankfully, I wasn't anti-God like my father was. I even credited the Supreme Being for granting me a few stellar traits that many people (be they children or grown-ups) seemed somewhat void of. I am a born idealist and I have always been a stickler regarding ethics and morality. In spite of my dad's poor example, I've always strived to do the right thing and made it a point to shun wrong-doing and deceitfulness and, within that framework, to be as fair and upstanding as I possibly could be.

With that deep-seated philosophy always in play (which, later, became my personal mantra), I've tried to be a staple and unwavering role-model. However, not only for my respective kids, but in the eyesight's of each and every child I was blessed to associate with throughout my life. And since I worked with and around high-school students for 34 years and drove a school bus for 6 years afterwards, the number of children I interacted with is virtually undeterminable.

Now, unequivocally, many people will totally dismiss me. They will say I'm dreaming, being unrealistic, accuse me of being "fake" and might even label me a "goody-two-shoes" (which, by the way, is a name I've been called before), but I wholeheartedly believe we are all in this thing together. I advocate that every adult man and woman should try their level best to be a stand-up (if not, stand-in) role-model in the eyes of every child they meet. To me, it should be S.O.P. (Standard Operational Procedure) and ever-present in the hearts and minds of every grown person.

In reality, you might very well adjudge yourself as the average "Joe" or "JoAnne." You might even say that you're having enough trouble trying to raise your own, biological children. "So why should I (you) concern myself with other people's kids and parental responsibilities?" you may ask.

I'd say that's a fair comment. "Let other folks worry about the well-being of their own kids," you might add. But what about that fabled child, the one "Whose got his own?" What about adopted children, stepchildren, foster kids, abandoned children and young people who silently lament their very existence? Do they matter at all? If you are an individual who is strongly opposed to the abortion premise (and some folks are downright fanatical about it), what about kids who are systematically aborted after they're conceived?

Believe me (although I'll be roundly criticized otherwise), I'm not passing judgment on anyone, but our country is in dire need of dedicated and admirable role-models. And it's absolutely farcical to expect heralded athletes or other famed individuals to rise to the occasion. Children are in need of tangible people.

It is not my intent to pat myself on the back when I divulge that I've loved and cherished adopted kids, a foster child, God-children and numerous surrogate kids but I regret not being able to touch and assist more of them.

Although my late wife entered our marital union with a biological son of her own, I never fathered a child of my own. That was rather ironic and disheartening too, especially since I envied my dad for siring seven sons. However, since my wife was unable to bear additional children within two years of our marriage (due to health problems), I was obliged to make due. I dearly loved my stepson and our father-son bond still thrives today. And, personally speaking, it was entirely out of the question that I'd engage in fathering a child outside of my marriage. That was always a bridge too far for me.

To my utter regret, my impact as a stellar role-model was somewhat limited. Because when I reflect back on the children I did manage to affect, whether they were African-American, Caucasian, Asian or other, I can rest assured that I was a "positive" influence in their young lives. And the precious memories I amassed while interacting with them have never subsided or died.

However, I am not severely scolding or faulting anyone for not sharing my idealistic beliefs. In reality, dealing with your own children is a challenging and time-consuming proposition. As a parent, you should be the primary and foremost molder of your child's emerging character and personality.

But if you're the kind of parent (or legal guardian) who subscribes to the theory of "Doing as I say" and not "Doing as I do,"

"THE SHAME OF IT ALL"

then you're well on the road of blatant hypocrisy and, oftentimes, future heartbreak. In essence, how can a person regard themselves as a role-model (or a fair-minded parent) when they persistently do not practice what they preach?

As I painstakingly pointed out, I was, alternately, fortunate when I was a child. After being exposed to somewhat of a "wash-out" as a parent (my physical father), I was awarded a surrogate dad, my esteemed uncle. And I've tried my level best to follow Uncle Bill's laid-out example and be a positive force in the lives of numerous children.

Naturally, I have no idea what kind of parent you (the reader) happen to be. Your personal dealings with children, in general, may rival or even eclipse mine. I would rousingly applaud you if that's the case. Then again, your individual parenting history might make my father's adverse actions look like a leisurely walk in the park. Only you, the singular person, knows the authentic truth.

But I feel compelled to cite the following: When I was young and was fortunate enough to have access to a black and white television set, I was able to watch a whole slew of moderately comical "sit-corns" on network TV. Whether it was "Leave It to Beaver," "Father Knows Best," or, maybe, "The Life of Riley" and "The Andy Griffith Show," (all of them, predominately white-oriented and starring white actors), they all showcased parents who were loving and supportive of their kids. For sure, the plots were relatively simple and the formats were somewhat superficial as well, but they left viewing audiences feeling optimistic and hopeful regarding the world around them.

Here, in the year 2020, cable and network television seems to be preoccupied with stark realism, explicit violence, sensationalism and so-called anti-heroes to the extent that even celluloid role-models have essentially vanished from the scene. I find that shameful and depressing because even pretend parents on film are, sometimes, better than deficient and wrong-headed parents in real-life homes.

However, in a period when black youth reportedly murder each other on a daily basis (especially in America's inner cities), when white teenagers periodically engage in bloody school massacres of fellow classmates and when child suicides are spiraling in proportion, we definitely do not need a despicable and insidious president like Donald John Trump to be head of our country.

Just when I was feeling that America was showing signs of moderate progress and marked change (a hypothesis that arose during Barack Obama's two-term presidency), a man like Trump was enthusiastically selected POTUS and I knew, right then and there, that chaos and untold despair was in the immediate offing. In the wake of Trump's 2016 election, my former glee was stopped cold and trampled on.

In retrospect, many remarks have been made about President Trump since he's occupied the Oval Office (the greater majority of them, derogatory). Amongst them, he's been called a habitual liar, a racist, a white supremacist, a misogynist and a sociopath but when I happened to hear a Caucasian male supporter suggest that he was a "role-model," I was tempted to hurl my remote control at my television set. In fact, the man's statement almost infuriated me as much as Rick Perry did when he audaciously deemed Trump as "the Chosen One."

Admittedly, I spoke to my TV during that particular incident (which is something I've habitually done for the past three years) and I addressed the man, asking, "What kind of father raised the likes of you? And what kind of men lived in your neighborhood when you were growing up? Al Capone? Paul - the Pimp? Jeffrey Dahmer? Perry - the Pervert? Jeffrey Epstein? Sal - the Serial Killer? Or, maybe, Drake - the Drug Czar? Who?

I really wanted to know, and in real time, what could have enticed that misguided man to make such a bizarre and asinine declaration? Was it in light of Trump's rather vague wealth or his elite status as our country's Chief Executive? What, on earth, was that man thinking about (or snorting) at that time and what awful horrors comprised his personal childhood? Enquiring minds, like mine, would have liked to have known.

All of that, I wondered about. And if you (the reader) happened to be on hand when that man voiced that endorsement, and you were in total agreement with him, I'm intrigued about your specific story also.

But, frankly, when I see children standing beside their parents at various Trump rallies, I emerge in awe of those instances too. For I do not know what goes on in the respective homes of his loyal supporters (or base) but I can assure you that no child in my personal orbit would ever be exposed to Trump's vulgar and unsavory rhetoric. Derogatory language like "sons-of-bitches," "bullshit," and "shithole countries" were never spoken in my home environment and I certainly wouldn't allow my kids to hear such language at a public assembly - and especially when it is loudly reverberating from the mouth of an individual who occupies the office of the Presidency of the United States of America. It is a sad and disgusting state of affairs when the most powerful man in the world boldly speaks like a crude and unabashed gutter rat.

Then again, maybe I'm missing the mark. Maybe I was being grossly unfair to the man who heralded the POTUS as a "role-model." After all, everything is about perception and perspective. And later on, when I fully focused on that man, I saw him in a different light. Not a benevolent or uplifting light, but a different light.

If there's one thing I've come to realize during my seventy-plus years in this world, it's that people generally adjudge other people by the way they, themselves, are. Meaning, after so many years of behaving and functioning like they customarily have done, they come to wholeheartedly believe that the next person operates in the same, exact fashion.

Briefly, allow me to cite you a personal example. In the tenth year of my marriage (I was actually married for 28 years), I was reluctantly engaged in a conversation with a longtime associate of mine at a local bar. The man was known to be unfaithful to his wife and was, seemingly, proud of it. I was aware of that factor, but I never verbally criticized him about it. First off, it wasn't my place and the man was big enough to do whatever he wanted to do. Secondly, he was about five years my senior and he was similar to most men I interacted with, whether they were black ones or white ones. Inwardly, I denounced marital infidelity but I was never an outspoken advocate against it. That explained my previous reluctance.

The relevant dialogue between me and my drinking buddy (we were sitting next to each other at the bar itself) got underway after he bought me a beer and graciously tipped the barmaid five dollars.

"I've gotta slow my damn roll, spending my dough," he spoke. "I've gotta save a wad of cash for my side piece. But- you know how that goes."

"Well.... I'll take your word for it," I casually replied.

Now, I have no idea what my comrade expected me to say, but he quickly took issue with what I did say.

"Take my word for it?" he mockingly offered. "Aw, I guess you don't have a babe or two on the sidelines, huh? A good looking dude like you?"

"Naw, not so far," I responded. "Being so-called "good looking," is that something that automatically makes guys mess around on their wives? Does that come with the territory?"

My comrade was visually taken aback. "Are you telling me, man, that you've never had an outside woman? Never? That's hard to believe!"

"I never saw the point of it," I spoke.

I soon regretted making the foregoing remark because it set my buddy off on a verbal tirade. "What are you, a damn monk or something?" he spoke. "You do like women, doncha? I mean - you're not a punk! How long you been married anyhow?"

Even in the midst of my associate losing his cool, I stayed quite calm, although he had tossed in a snide insult about my manhood,

"THE SHAME OF IT ALL"

I wasn't miffed at him. "I've been married a little over ten years," I told him, "and I happen to love my wife. Otherwise, I wouldn't have married her."

"Shit, I've been married twenty-two years," he proudly announced. "Well - I'll give you a couple of more years or more and you'll be on board, just like the rest of us. Mark my damn words. Variety is the spice of life, my man."

Essentially, that ended that particular conversation. In all probability, I could have talked until I was blue in the face and I would have never made headway with my womanizing pal. And neither would he have changed my mind. In fact, I could have told him I had been married twenty or thirty years and he still would have given me a "couple of more years." Sometimes, it is best to "table" certain verbal disputes. Meaning, just agree to disagree. It'll save a lot of wear and tear.

At this juncture, one might ask, "What does the foregoing "bar" episode have to do with the Donald Trump supporter who exalted the President as a "role model?" Well, merely this: It is very possible that my personal definition of a role-model might be entirely different from that of the man I elected to take issue with. Specifically speaking, the qualities that man admired in a role-model may have been diametrically opposite mine.

After all, he was a Caucasian man and I'm an African-American man. People may accuse me of being preoccupied with race, or even say I begrudge white folks in general, but we cannot get around it, racial biasness and animus is more than commonplace in our country. Therefore, since the President has become somewhat of a standard-bearer for that kind of age-old behavior, it could partially be a reason why that singled-out white man endorsed Trump as a role-model.

I purposely used the term "partially" because there are a whole gamut of traits Donald Trump displays (either overtly or undercover) that individuals of questionable character might deem admirable in our President. And I chose to use the word "traits" rather than "qualities" because the latter term references a degree of merit and high-standard.

But it's a character trait (or flaw) when an individual consistently engages in verbally disparaging or belittling other people (specifically, his critics), when he or she constantly lies and stonewalls, when a person callously spews out racist jargon, when they brag about grabbing women by their private parts, when they disdain the news media and when they endorse and practice bullying tactics. And all of the foregoing acutely defines Donald Trump to the very hilt.

Therefore, it is quite possible, and I hope I'm in error, but it is conceivable that the man whom I took issue with is on the same page (morally-wise) that the POTUS is on. So, in his viewpoint, Trump could be a role-model to him.

When I take the time to look back upon my long and eventful life, there's something about me that exceedingly differs me from most of the people I've known, and especially when I focus on my black brothers and sisters. To be specific, I am virtually unshockable when it comes to what white racist either "say" or "do."

The greater majority of individuals of that particular ilk were weaned and nurtured on racial hatred and, eventually, they will go to their graves as die-hard racist also. I have long become expectant and practically immune and numb to their putrid and sick ideology and behavior.

I vividly recall my maternal grandmother, speaking to her daughter (my mother), stating, "Things will be much better for the colored folks of this world when the prejudice and hateful white folks die out." However, even though my mom was the optimist I priorly acknowledged, she soon responded and almost instantaneously burst Grandma's bubble by saying, "But, Mamma, they teach their babies every day that God sends to be just like they are."

At that time, I had no inkling of what my granny and mamma was talking about (hell - I was around five or six years old at

"THE SHAME OF IT ALL"

the time). Therefore, I just walked away, giving their remarks little thought. But several years later, I seriously mulled over their conversation and managed to empathize with both of them. I sympathized with my grandmother for her feeling of "hopefulness" and I credited my mother for her "discernment."

Not so coincidentally, but that same, yesteryear verbal exchange between my mom and my grandmother invaded my mind back in early 2019. It wasn't so much about the race component (my grandma, similar to many elderly people of her generation, truly believed that God would, someday, banish racism altogether), but I had long aligned myself with my mother's comment of dissent. Mom maintained that racial animus was traditionally passed down from parent to child, and on a daily basis.

So, in 2019, when I saw a filmed news clip of former Attorney-General Jeff Sessions speaking in front of an assembly of grinning high school students (all of them, seemingly Caucasian) and heard them boisterously and continuously shouting, "Lock her up!," I was immediately appalled and disgusted. However, when I observed the glee on the face of A.G. Sessions, I was, not in the least bit, surprised. In my estimation, the man was hand-plucked from the legendary "swamp" by Donald Trump himself.

But my mind soon zeroed-in on those high school teenagers and, in spite of them being white, I felt real shame for them and their home-residing parents as well. Then, after about a half an hour, I thought about an experiment, and one which would be compatible with the ongoing learning process and would test that group's knowledge and writing skills.

The following is the premise for my self-concocted, hypothetical experiment and it's quite simple, really. It would entail an adult escorting each student who attended that rousing assembly to a secluded area, reasonably away from any fellow teenagers, and provide him (or her) with a pencil and a sheet of lined paper. Then, instruct them to adhere to the forthcoming guidelines, but entirely disallow them to telephone home or to use any electronic devices.

UP-CLOSE AND PERSONAL

The instructions are as follows: (And I'll verbally stipulate them, as though I'm addressing one of the subject students).

"Firstly, on the sheet of paper you have before you, I'd like for you, to the best of your ability, answer this question: Why do you feel that Hillary Clinton, who was formerly a candidate for the President of the United States, deserves to be "locked up?" And, please, list the respective crime or crimes she committed, which would warrant her incarceration."

"And, secondly, after completing the first part of your assignment, then flip your paper over to the other side and write down your personal impression of what it means to be, quote, "locked up." What, in your opinion, does a locked up or jailed person go through?"

Now, you (the reader) might berate such a hypothetical assignment. You might dismiss it, calling it stupid or absurd. And if you happen to be an adult Caucasian person, you may not have the faintest idea how to answer the questions that were posed during my imaginary examination. That's just one of the many rewards of white privileged. It is said that, "Ignorance is bliss," but in so many, many instances, having white skin is bliss also. Unless a Caucasian citizen is involved in a crime that demands their subsequent arrest, the majority of them goes through life without ever seeing the inside of a jail cell. And that applies to white youths too, even the ones who loudly yearned for Hillary Clinton's unfair incarceration. (During my long ago youth, I was arrested at least five times for W.W.B. (walking while black), although the white racist cops labelled it "peace disturbance").

In spite of all the yelling and ugly fanfare about Hillary Clinton being arrested and jailed, it never came to pass. It was all hype and nasty hoopla. And here, in the year 2020, she was completely cleared and exonerated. But I have a relevant question to pose, a question that's directed at Donald Trump's loyal base, and especially the ones who nightly and daily called for imprisoning

"THE SHAME OF IT ALL"

the former Secretary-of-State. And they joyously continued their verbal assault well-after the presidential election.

Here is my query: "After you methodically implanted the seeds of disdain in the minds of your respective off springs and, then, proceeded to water and fertilize them (and I'm certain Hillary didn't stand alone), will you now go back, admit your error and unearth those seeds?"

You can brand me audacious and impudent, but I'll take the liberty to answer my own question. I'm more than sure that your response is an emphatic, NO! It's because so many of Trump's die-hard followers are exactly like him (cut from the very same cloth). For example: When it was proof-positive that the POTUS was totally wrong about the "birther" issue regarding Barack Obama, he reluctantly conceded with a subdued and somewhat tepid "Yes." Then, afterwards, he never revisited his debunked theory about the former black President of the United States, and even when his loyal supporters opted to breathe new life into it. That's the Donald John Trump I've come to know and disparage.

At this juncture, that is all I have to say about Mr. Trump's many deficiencies. However, in my continuous audacity, I am poised to say one more thing to individuals who are still in the parenting arena, and especially those who occasionally plant seeds. If you are longing to reap an abundant and fruitful harvest someday, then I pray that you purchase seed packets labelled "Benevolent," "Righteousness" and "Love." Otherwise, you may very well inherit life's weeds and shrubbery at the end of the day. In the final analysis, it's all up to you, the individual.

"THE ART OF BEING FOOLISH"

I'VE BEEN AN AFRICAN-AMERICAN MY entire, long life and, therefore, it stands to reason that I've interacted with mostly fellow African-Americans (or black folks) throughout my life. Okay, before you lambaste me for declaring such an asinine and nonsensical fact, allow me to redeem myself in real time and real color.

Since I am, indeed, black and quite senior also, I have spent the vast majority of my days (and nights) in the company of people who look somewhat like me. Admittedly, I'm totally unaware of what transpires in traditional white homes in America; either on the surface or behind closed doors, but I have extensive insight and knowledge when the focus is on African-American households.

I've known multiple black men and women who held down two, different jobs, trying to make financial ends meet. And I've also known various women and men who worked credible and so-called "good-paying" jobs and many of them, still, had difficulty staying above financial flood waters. Unfortunately, even in modern times, black people still lag behind our white counterparts wage-wise.

So, when I suggest that black households in general (especially ones that contain and sustain children) are virtually living from paycheck to paycheck, I am not knocking my fellow brothers and sisters, I'm just emphasizing an age-old condition. Black people have always struggled financially in this country.

However, it is not my primary desire to take issue with the continuous wage-gap between white and black workers in America.

"THE ART OF BEING FOOLISH"

Instead, and, probably, surprising to you (the reader), it's explicitly about a faraway foreign country that's known as "Ukraine," which thus far (in the midst of a brand new year) has played a major role in the impeachment of President Donald J. Trump.

At this particular moment in time, the final verdict is still up in the air. Trump may emerge essentially unscathed, with just a slight slap on his wrist. And I haven't the foggiest idea about the end game.

But what caught my eye about the whole scandalous affair is this: Personally, I am much inclined to believe that the President is guilty of practically everything he is accused of doing, and much, much more. For an individual who is, apparently, void of scruples and integrity is capable of all kinds of tomfoolery and graft.

However, what bothers me the most about the POTUS is that he thoroughly believes that the American public is collectively dumb, stupid and gullible. For example: When Trump appeared on nationwide television late last year and proudly announced he decided to not lob (or fire) a retaliatory missile at a foreign country because it would kill or harm a number of "innocent" people (civilians), he genuinely thought the listening and viewing public believed him.

Well, maybe, his lockstep base bought into his claim, but I credit the greater majority of Americans with a quality known as "discernment" and that select group, in their hearts, are well-aware that Trump is - and has always been completely barren of any degree of human compassion. If the Chief Executive cares about anyone who's outside of his immediate family and his political orbit, where is the proof of it? Sorrowfully, there is none! Even the latter group, his political allies and cronies, are expendable and are subject to be thrown under the Trump bus at any given moment.

However, being the TV personality he actually is, the POTUS thrives on publicity and illuminated notoriety. Therefore, he wanted to be seen as a magnanimous hero when he talked about not launching that missile.

To be frank, I immediately laughed when he voiced his decision to "stand-down." Not because he said something that I found amusing, but because of what popped up in mind at that time. As clear as a bell, I could hear "Mighty Mouse" singing, "Here I come to save the day!"

And that was the President's chief goal, you know? He is so phony and disingenuous it's a crying shame. Like, when he was still on the campaign trail and opted to address the African-American population. He asked, "What do you have to lose?" In reality, Donald Trump doesn't care one iota, and has never cared about the fate and well-being of black people in this country or any other country, for that matter. He does, however, want "our" votes come election time. As to what "we" had to lose, I urge you to seriously think about the numerous so-called "conservative" federal Judges Donald Trump has appointed so far, as well as the Republican-led assault on "voter-registration" and "polling procedures." And those are just for starters. Let us not overlook Trump "minions" like Mitch McConnell. If Hillary Clinton was in the Oval Office, we could successfully contend with Obama-haters such as him. And, please, keep a watchful eye on McConnell's racist agenda also.

Here, in late January of 2020, a recent poll maintained that eighty-three percent of America's black citizens believe our President is a racist. Although I hate to admit it (and I'm aware that African-Americans are not monolithic when it comes to mind-sets), I am not surprised regarding the polling feelings of the other seventeen percent of blacks.

During my 75 years on this earth I've dealt with a vast array of fellow black people and, to my grief, I've even known a few of "us" who would join the "Ku Klux Klan" if they were allowed membership. Now, some people might find that remark amusing or absurd, but it's not. It's sad and tragic! But far too many of my brethren and sisters are afflicted with maladies such as "self-loathing," "white-envy" and "white-lust" as well.

In actuality, there's nothing mysterious or bizarre about the aforementioned maladies (or mind-sets), especially when it comes to young black Americans. They are all by-products of age-old white conditioning and subtle brainwashing.

In my, admittedly, homespun opinion, when we (as parents) allow our children to sit in front of a TV set day-in and day-out and they are, subsequently, bombarded and saturated with the feats and actions of Caucasian heroes and/or Caucasian heroines, we inadvertently set ourselves up to be made to deal with a number of mixed-up, misguided and brainwashed children. Many of them long to be what they see. It's not remotely the fault of black children, however.

It's not even a knock on African-American parents. They enjoy providing their kids sources of entertainment and that's commendable, to a certain extent. (It's not so wise, though, to allow your TV set to become an electronic baby-sitter).

In the final analysis, however, the black dilemma in America comes down to us being an oppressed and downtrodden race in this country. Many children are void of an authentic identity and, inwardly, they loathe the identity they do have. And that's why we're in dire need of upstanding and tangible role-models.

But more than anything else, black children desperately need to know from "whence" they came. To me, it's like beating a dead horse, but I have long advocated that if African-American history was incorporated into school curriculums (even in predominately Caucasian schools), it would "socially" educate black and white students alike.

Unfortunately though, that's another book, another controversial issue and a different topic of discussion as well. The current subject at hand is Donald John Trump and a country in the news that's called "Ukraine." But in a very significant way, it's relevant to being black in America also. Over the years, I had the opportunity to associate with minimal white families (most of them, well-to-do) and they had little or no idea of what it meant to be "poor" or to financially struggle from day-to-day. Maybe, it was because I was mostly around long-time high school teachers who were paid quite well.

To my knowledge, it's indisputable that there's a notable wealth gap between black and white citizens in this nation. So, it's not surprising that the two races view monetary matters differently too. Therefore, when Donald Trump and his vocal henchmen attempted to minimize or "water down" the overall importance of Ukraine receiving the previously promised four hundred million dollars, it became a key point of contention. Maybe, not for you (the reader) or the average Caucasian person either, but certainly for me and many black people I've known throughout the years.

Almost instantly, I put myself in the place of the people of Ukraine and its government too, and I personalized it. Since I have periodically found myself living from pay-check to paycheck, I felt the pain and anxiety that accompanies such dire and trying circumstances. In my life, I had to face due and overdue gas and electric bills, I found myself out of food occasionally and my automobile, unexpectedly, has broken down from time to time. And that's not the end of my personal scenario. I have also found myself barren of monetary savings on occasions and had no means of procuring any substantial funds elsewhere. Therefore, during those very hard and trying periods, if my weekly or bi-weekly paycheck had been delayed or lost altogether, I would have been in a financial bind that would have been almost catastrophic!

None of the above is farfetched or, in any degree, fictionalized, and especially in the lives of people who live from paycheck to paycheck and, hopefully, you are not one of those individuals. However, I also hope you're not beyond sympathizing or emphasizing with people who have to reckon with comparable or even worse ordeals. So, when we return our focus to the foreign country of Ukraine, it's not at all difficult to imagine their former position either. Ukraine was in desperate need of that pre-approved assistance from the United States. They anxiously anticipated it and had specific plans regarding it. Therefore, when it was held back

"THE ART OF BEING FOOLISH"

for nefarious reasons, Ukraine, too, was in an insidious position. I can't refrain from wondering how many Ukrainians suffered in the wake of Trump's self-serving delay. Also, how many Ukraine soldiers were injured or even killed due to the withholding of arms and weaponry? And lastly, and certainly not least, what on earth will our reckless and corrupt POTUS do next?

I can't speak for my fellow Americans (many of us are good at saying, "I don't have a dog in the race"), but I wonder about all of the aforestated and more. And when Trump and his cohorts casually but arrogantly tried to brush off the entire Ukraine controversy by mouthing, "No harm-no foul," I was virtually livid!

Like I said before, I can't gauge how "John Q. Public" views the state of affairs in America since Trump took the oath of office, but I often become highly incensed when he and his surrogates obviously sees us all as damn fools! The President seems to believe if he says something over and over again, the citizenry of America will, inevitably, believe him. And sadly and evidently, there's an inordinate group of people who have succumbed to his philosophy, but I'm surely not one of them.

Thus far, in January of 2020, the media has accredited the POTUS with over 15,000 lies (or falsehoods) since he's been in office and even if one-fifth of them are vividly disclosed, coming from his own mouth or are verifiable "tweets" he sent out, it is scandalous and shameful. If the man was the fictional "Pinocchio" and was standing at the entrance to D.C.'s White House, he has lied so frequently that he would have to dispatch a Secret Service agent to the state of Virginia to blow his runny nose.

Sure, that's a gross exaggeration and my attempt to display my inborn sense of humor. But even in the midst of my ongoing anger and contempt for our so-called Chief Executive, I cannot resist making light of him sometimes. It, in many ways, safeguards my sanity.

For instance, when Trump's mouthpieces flippingly tried to explain away the "Hunter and Joe Biden extortion deal" by asserting that the President was actually fighting corruption in Ukraine, I found myself thinking about a Jim Carrey movie entitled "Liar, Liar."

Maybe you've seen that movie or maybe you did not, but, in it, Carrey has a comical scene wherein he goes into a public restroom and commences to beat the holy hell out of himself. So, when I heard Trump defenders state he was "fighting corruption in Ukraine," I pictured the POTUS doing the very same thing. In essence, I imagined him going in the Oval Office alone, then locking all the doors and furiously beating the living daylights out of himself. In my viewpoint, he would truly be fighting corruption then.

But there was a serious component to that concocted lie too, one that donned on me right away. The country of Ukraine had long struggled with political corruption and graft. They had addressed it, wrestled with it and even elected a new president in the wake of it all. *Zelensky* was the man's name and, on the surface, he seemed to be a decent, dedicated and upstanding man. However, that didn't stop Trump and his minions (among them, Rudy Giuliani) from embroidering him into their seedy and nefarious fabric. When Zelensky was obliged to step forward and declare that he was completely unaware (and, seemingly, unconcerned) of the held-up multi-million dollar support package, he was forcefully pulled into Trump's corruption-ladened orbit. My empathy and heart goes out to the Ukrainian president. Because in knowing how vindictive our POTUS is, and supposing, too that he'd be reelected in the fall of 2020, Zelensky had no other recourse but to lie.

Sometimes, I feel like the average American citizen's vision is 20-10 and I, personally, see 20-20 and can see miles in the distance. I'm not being braggadocious or haughty. It's just that I seem to view things at its core value, and with no frills attached. With that said, I want to convey to you something that has been ever-present on my mind since the Ukraine scandal came into prominence shortly after the "whistle blower" stepped forward and shined a light on it.

"THE ART OF BEING FOOLISH"

First and foremost, I instantly and wholeheartedly believed the whistle blower was being entirely honest and aboveboard. In essence, he was reporting that Donald J. Trump, with the aid of his henchmen and loyalist, was holding back an already-appropriated aid package for the country of Ukraine, and in exchange for political damage and dirt on the one man (Joe Biden) who Trump perceived as a formidable Democratic challenger in the 2020 presidential election.

I wasn't remotely surprised by the whistle blower's charges and cannot begin to comprehend why others (including members of Trump's cult-like base) could dispute the "accusers" validity. And after so many people came forward and corroborated the whistle blower's story, I have never understood exactly why the President and his angry constituents insisted upon knowing the identity of the whistle blower either. What would that "outing" accomplish? Manage to scare and frighten all future whistle blowers into staying muzzled and silent? And what would the Republican Party do to the Ukraine whistle blower if he or she stood before them, throw darts at him or her? Or, even worse, execute the person?

In stark reality, Donald Trump is a petty, begrudging and jealous-hearted man (Barack Obama is proof-positive of the latter). Therefore, it comes to no surprise that he strongly desired to publicly denounce and punish the individual who blew the whistle on his unsavory and deceitful behavior in the Ukraine controversy.

However, what agitated me even more was the shameful way Trump and his allies (all of them, Republicans) extended their slanderous rhetoric and naked fury to include seasoned and dedicated government employees (people like Maria Yovanavich and William Taylor) who had the courage to step forward and tell "the truth, and nothing but the truth," regarding their knowledge of the Ukraine affair.

That was, to me, the epitome of vindictiveness and unvarnished evil. And I strongly believe that is so - because I had soldiered for three years in the United States army and was also employed at a government facility not long after my separation from service.

Personally, I worked under the supervision of a man named "Russell Dunham," who was a recipient of the Congressional Medal of Honor, and he was an individual of character, integrity and principle, and so was I. In my federal job, and every job I held afterwards, I amassed an impressive work record and I took great pride in my execution of my work duties. You can call me naive or whatever, but I saw the government employees who testified in those 2019 hearings in the very same light.

However, I also saw something else, something that was more alarming. Right before my eyes, I witnessed a gradual metamorphosis. I saw the Republican Party (which was once the party of Ronald Reagan), with no feeling of remorse or misgivings, transform into the "TRUMPLICAN" party and that is where they are today. They are collectively exempt of integrity, moral aptitude, ethics and basic honesty. They, just like the pseudo-god they've come to worship, namely Donald J. Trump, will "say" and "do" anything to preserve and shore up their political positions and have no authentic regards for the overall well-being of the American public.

That is more than apparent when they remain idle while our President boldly tramples over the United States Constitution, when they allow him to constantly poke holes into our moral curtain and when they fiercely defend and rubber stamp "any" and "every" shady scheme he engages in.

The POTUS has frequently insisted, that as President, he "can do anything he wants to do." And although that claim once sounded absurd and ridiculous too, at present, with the endorsement and full backing of the Trumplican party, the President's boast has become fact.

Hearkening back to something Rick Perry put forth, when he proudly proclaimed the POTUS as "the Chosen One," I can also visualize the living God's omniscient wisdom in the matter and I offer Him my sincere homage. As I previously stated, I took firm exception to Mr. Perry's outrageous claim and perceived Trump, instead, as the "selected one." I knew, for sure, the Supreme Being was in the equation and I was relatively certain also that He had no intent whatsoever to uplift a man of ill-repute and indecency (such as Trump) to a status that would warrant adoration and prominence. And upon clearly understanding that God really does "work in mysterious ways," I came to realize an alternate revelation. I saw it as a God-inspired act to lift the blinders from the collective eyes of our nation's populace. In retrospect, if Donald John Trump had not won the presidency, the average American (and the world at-large) would not have known how self-serving, corrupt, shameless and Satan-inspired the greater majority of our political leaders really are. In addition, we became cognizant that the so-called "swamp" was always in existence and its vile creatures were forever lurking and in an attacking mold, but we were basically unaware of it. Owing to the current POTUS and his emulating cohorts, the age-old blinders are no longer there. In essence, "I was blind and now I see."

"THE BULLY BEHIND THE PULPIT"

WHEN I SET OUT TO write this book and the one that preceded it, which was entitled "Racism, Sexism, Trumpism, Pseudo-Christianity and the Cinema," I found myself reflecting on some wise words of advice that my dear mother passed on to me when I was a mere child. She often told me (as well as my quartet of brothers), "If you can't say something nice or positive, then don't say anything at all." Although I can't speak for any of my siblings, I attached great merit to Mom's advice and practically swallowed it "hook, line and sinker," but to a certain extent. As I aged, I even took the liberty to apply addendums to my mother's words of wisdom. I made a promise to myself that I would live my life, trying my level best not to trample over the feelings of other people. And, not to be flip, I saw children as people too.

I was adamant about that self-imposed promise and I, eventually, opted to add a provision to it also. I realized my idealism was in play, but I made, yet, an additional vow, saying, "As I interact with people throughout my day, if they are having a lousy or trying day - like we all do from time to time, I will not be at fault for making his or her day even worse.

From the word "say-go," I knew that was a tall order to fill, but still I tried, and I've continued to try till this very day. People go through so much in this life, all the disappointments, despair and heartaches, and unless we are literally walking in their shoes, we have no idea how they feel physically or mentally. A once popular song suggested that we, "Try a Little Tenderness" and that has always been my underlying goal when I dealt with the average Joe or JoAnne.

However, sometimes a person of principle has no other recourse but to go off-script and when it comes to a despicable and caustic man like Donald Trump, I feel compelled to speak up. Trump's horrendous conduct and deplorable actions are the driving forces behind my writing efforts and I pray that they will, someday, make an impact upon people who love justice and unredacted peace as well.

Although the title of this particular chapter foretells what it's basically about, it's not explicitly about the cruel and intimidating style of the POTUS, and it is not written, remotely hoping for any semblance of moral reform or a change of attitude. Sorrowfully, Trump will always be Trump and just like his overt stance on racism, his bullying persona is well-embedded in his heart as well.

But, I still maintain that there's life after President Trump and there was life before Donald Trump too. And with that said, I'd like to reflect on a specific happening that occurred well before I knew such a vile human being like Mr. Trump existed, but all in a sincere desire to touch the hearts and minds of others, and especially young people who may be absent of discernment and mature reasoning.

In my personal reflection, I was at the tender age of 25 when I embarked upon my 34 year employment trek with the St. Louis, Mo. Public Schools. As I acknowledged before, I always worked with students who were on the high school level. Throughout the years, I served in the capacity of a Business Manager (though it was officially labelled as a "Book clerk-treasurer," which allowed the St. Louis Board of Education to pay out a more modest salary) and, therein, I had my own office. I had attended a couple of business-administration schools while in the military, so I was in my league and was confident I would be successful in my work role.

However, I wasn't so confident or enthused when I was apprised of what "types" of teenagers I was slated to deal with regarding my very first work assignment with the Board of Education. When I highlighted types, it was my personal assessment, and it had little to do with race or gender. Mostly it had everything to do with a word spelled "i-n-c-o-r-r-i-g-i-b-l-e," incorrigible.

To be frank, I had never heard that rather harsh word attached to any other racial group except African-American, of which I'm a proud member. And since the school was, indeed, a high school (grades 9 through 12), it accommodated mostly black teenaged boys and girls. I took the initiative to say "mostly" because after working at the site for nearly two years (it was originally called "Opportunity High School" and, then, the "Abraham Lincoln High School), I could count the number of Caucasian enrollees by using the fingers of my two hands. The school's enrollment capacity was around 250 and, therefore, the white students who did wind up there stuck out like sore thumbs.

By academic design, our school was in the offing for delinquent and misbehaving kids, along with children who were struggling with the standard curriculum at traditional high schools and, some, who were generally disinterested in academics altogether. I studied and carefully scrutinized the student body on a daily basis and never did I see a youngster who was entirely uncontrollable or beyond reform. Maybe, it was because I happened to be black myself and I knew we all had our personal demons to ward off. That was, and has always been, commonplace with black folks in America. Therefore, the term "incorrigible" was another word concocted by the white establishment, designed to diminish the worth of African-Americans. Unless he or she is an out-and-out sociopath, no child in any race is unsalvageable or a complete lost cause.

In stark reality, the scarcity of white enrollees regarding our school was credited directly to the Caucasian power structure too. When black students were suspended or expelled from any high school in our district, they were given no other alternative than

"THE BULLY BEHIND THE PULPIT"

to either attend our school, physically drop-out or study for their high school equivalency (which was called a G.E.D.).

However, by complete contrast, when Caucasian students were ousted from predominantly-white high schools (for any rationale), they were permitted to enroll in other predominantly-white high schools. Therefore, even unruly and delinquent Caucasian students were favored and emboldened in the name of racial biasness.

In my estimation, the forestated was par for the course and nothing that I had not seen before. Even in the United States army, I went head-to-head with racism and blatant white privilege. But, still, I felt a degree of sympathy for the white youngsters who did happen to attend our school. And it wasn't because they were picked on, bullied or ostracized (if any of them were, I never witnessed it), it was basically because they individually looked so lonely and, sometimes, lost.

There was a standard joke that was shared between me and my fellow black co-workers at the school (teachers, custodians, clerical staff, etc.), a moderately amusing and light-hearted comment that emerged when we sighted a lone Caucasian youngster who was walking around the school building. Someone would say, "I wonder who had it in for him (or her). What bigwig in the downtown office was so pissed off at his (or her) parents, it got them banished to here?"

For a short while, I, too, laughed but when one of my male cohorts rather gloatingly remarked, "He's what they call po' (or poor) white trash, can't ya' tell?" I was no longer amused. In fact, I eventually bonded with the very same white boy who was smeared by my co-worker. In my opinion, the young boy was relatively poor, and he was, indeed, white as well, but he wasn't "trash" or anything resembling that unkind put-down. His name was "Daniel" and I fondly list him as one of my many surrogate brothers or sons. There is a meaningful story that encompasses my long ago relationship with Danny, but it is not pertinent at this precise juncture. However, I do wish to shift my focus to a male student, two of them, actually, but neither of them was white and neither of them was affiliated with my yesteryear social circle either. Until this very day, I deeply regret that factual omission. I might have been a sobering voice.

But, please, allow me to backtrack for a minute or so. Before I embark upon my scenario about the two young men I alluded to, permit me to cite an incident which might grant you (the reader) a genuine insight about our school.

The brick building we were housed in was relatively small, especially for a high school. It had three floors, no elevators or escalators, and contained approximately twenty classrooms, that were predominantly situated on the second and third floors. However, two of the classrooms were located on the first floor, along with the Main Office, the Principal's Office and the school cafeteria which, sometimes, served as an auditorium.

We had custodians, cafeteria workers, a couple of Counselors, a Social Worker, a Nurse but only one Security Officer and most of them were situated on the first floor. My business office, however, was on the second floor.

As I indicated earlier, I was 25 when I began working for the Board of Education and, therein, I was physically fit, able-bodied, and agile and wasn't intimidated by any student or adult in the building. That assertion might strike you as somewhat strange but I said it because, on some occasions, I was obliged to take on the role of a security guard, especially when the assigned officer was nowhere to be found. The following is one of those occasions: One afternoon, I happened to be on the third floor and, while walking down the hallway, a fist fight between two black male students broke out in a nearby classroom. And since a woman was the teacher, she was standing back, looking awestruck.

I, on the other hand, was a man and without a moment's delay, I inserted myself into the fracas and, soon, it was squelched. I, then, instructed the disputing young men to keep silent and trail

"THE BULLY BEHIND THE PULPIT"

me down to the Principal's office and they complied. I had no idea as to why they were fighting and I didn't inquire.

But when the three of us reached the second floor landing, just minutes later, we came upon two black girls who were fiercely battling in the corridor. Shaking my head in disgust, I instantly meshed myself into that conflict too. I calmed the young ladies down, even as they cussed and taunted each other, and, soon, they joined my pilgrimage also. Then, I was escorting four students to the Principal's Office.

Now, one might think it was smooth sailing from that point on, but it wasn't! When me and my entourage set a collective foot on the first floor and rounded the corner that would grant us access to the Principal's Office, another brawl was in full progress. However, it was a horse of a different color (that, too, was another one of my mother's adages). This time, however, instead of a physical confrontation between two high school students, this one involved an angry teenaged girl and a tenured female teacher. They were also African-American but that was a mere afterthought. I would have been just as appalled and just as livid if that black girl had had the gall to attack a Caucasian teacher, female or male.

Within mere seconds, I grabbed the aggressive girl by her forearm, preventing her from landing a blow on the teacher. I said, "You need to calm down, young lady!" However, instead of heeding my advice, the girl wielded a balled up fist and solidly punched me in my chest area. And I mean "hard," just as if she was a trained boxer!

That actually caught me off guard. Due to my father's brutalizing actions when it came to my mom, I had vowed to never hit a female. Evidently, that promise was away on holiday at that precise moment because, instantaneously, I retaliated in kind. Using the back of my opened hand, I struck the girl across her face and sent her sprawling to the floor.

To be honest, I was still seething and somewhat furious in the brief aftermath of that harrowing episode. And even when the Principal appeared on the scene and took the initiative to help the downed young lady back to her feet, I still struggled to regain my composure. Alternately though, I regretted I had lost my temper and I inwardly admonished myself. But about an hour later, when the school's Principal paid a visit to my office and offered me some sincere advice about the foregoing episode, I balked at it. The Principal suggested that, if a Board official came forward to ask me about my snap reaction during the fracas, I should indicate it was my way of squelching her "hysteria." (I imagined my boss had seen too many movies). However, with little thought, I replied, "No, Sir, I won't say that. That girl had the nerve to punch me and I hit her back. Case-closed. She's lucky I chose not to use my fist, I might have broken her darn jaw."

To be completely candid, the foregoing expose was just a small sampling of what our school was really about. In my opinion, the white powers-that-be (the select group who conceived our school) didn't actually care about the teenagers who would, alternately, attend our facility. They just desired to keep those "African-American" kids off the streets of Saint Louis for seven or eight hours during the week days.

Undoubtedly, I was always suspicious and skeptical of the underlying motives of Caucasian people in power, and especially when it came to black Americans. But upon referencing a 1940's film entitled "They Made Me a Criminal," I could relate. If I tend to come across as "obsessively" skeptical, then my white brothers and sisters fostered my skepticism.

Even if some of our school's founders were totally exempt of racial biasness or discrimination, I questioned their discernment in the matter. In my viewpoint, common sense would convey that when you lump together a bunch of like-minded bitter and disruptive individuals and house them inside a designated site (a school, a prison, etc.), you are asking for continuous strife, conflict and anarchy. Many of our underprivileged, poor and begrudging kids were trying to "out-bad" their fellow students, all in an effort to be noticed and achieve a real significance in this life.

Every teacher and staff member who worked at that school, especially the black ones, knew we were fighting a losing battle but, still, we tried our level best. If we could touch a single kid, convince him or her that their current situation was only temporary and a passing phase, we could have achieved a personal significance ourselves. Regretfully, those kind of triumphs were far and in between. Therefore, during the time that we were employed at that so-called "alternative school," we secretly regarded ourselves as frustrated, but well-paid babysitters and, sometimes, untrained police officers.

Upon looking back at the times I spent at that rather unique high school, which, again, was my very first work assignment for the Saint Louis Public Schools, there are many memories that flood my mind. Some of them, outlandish; some of them, lighthearted and comical and some of them, downright foreboding, tragic and purely unforgettable.

It's that latter premise, "purely unforgettable," that comes to mind as I refocus on the two male students I alluded to earlier, right before I made an effort to familiarize you (the reader) with the kind of school I worked at. Those two black youngsters, in more ways than the obvious (meaning race), almost typified the male enrollees at our facility.

One of the subject boys was named William Mason and, not surprising, was called "Billy" around the school house. He was considered to be nice looking, fashionable, outgoing and, not common to our type of school, highly intelligent. In fact, if you conversed with some of his classroom teachers (black ones and white ones), you would likely assume Billy was an oddity or a misfit at our facility.

But that was the initial impression a person might have of Billy, myself included. However, as time eventually showed, he was a misleading read. William Mason not only ran with a bunch of trouble-making ruffians, he appeared to be their unofficial leader. I imagined they admired him for his intellect and savvy. Eventually, I came to see him as a bully and I surmised, maybe, it was a ploy to downplay his academic qualities and be considered as just "one of the boys" instead, rendering him rough-edged, defiant and tough. Obviously, it was that behavior attitude that led to his suspension from a traditional high school.

Then, came a young man named Kirk Jones who, like Billy Mason, was also an African-American enrollee at our school. Kirk was small-statured, average looking, soft-spoken, seemed to have a sparse wardrobe and, apparently, was a loner. So, totally unlike Billy Mason, he had no support group in his midst and mostly kept to himself.

Kirk Jones might have been fine at a regular high school, but at our rather unorthodox facility, where teenaged show-offs and thugs went to great lengths to "out-bad" fellow bad boys and garner a so-called "reputation" while doing so, he was at a daily risk. Not at risk of peril or grave danger, but of juvenile antics and unprovoked taunting.

Apparently, in Billy Mason's opinion, Kirk was a "punk," a "sissy," and a "chump" and any other derogatory put-down he could verbally muster up. But to add insult to injury, Billy wasn't satisfied with only vocally poking fun at Kirk. So, he upped his antagonizing game by physically slapping Kirk on the back of his head and pushing him around whenever he saw fit. And when Billy was around his amused and edging-on cohorts, Billy often "saw fit" during those occasions.

It was bad enough that Kirk Jones was subjected to Billy Mason's bullying in and around the school building but it was apparent that the two of them lived near each other also, maybe in the very same neighborhood. I never knew for sure about that but when they made their afternoon departures from the school and then proceeded to catch the exact same Bi-State bus which was heading towards north St. Louis, I assumed it was somewhat true.

Therefore, since quite a few of Billy's running buddies boarded that same northbound bus also, it stood to reason that the teasing and taunting (and, probably, the head-slapping too), frequently occurred on those daily bus treks also.

Tragically and regretfully, I was right on the money about my assumption. One morning Kirk came to school and obviously had had enough of Billy's repetitious bullying conduct. The taunting must have been ongoing throughout that particular school day, but that was never verified.

Again, I made an educated assumption because I learned several days later that Kirk had periodically stated he was "sick and tired" of Billy's harassment and head-slaps and he was going to kill Billy. I purposely indicated that Kirk had "periodically" voiced that threat solely because it was revealed later on that Kirk had pre-shared his deadly vow with a number of classroom teachers.

Evidently though, none of those teachers took Kirk at his word. They didn't bother to sound the alarm bell to the school's Principal, to the assigned Security Officer or even to the school's Social Worker. Obviously, they gave no merit whatsoever to Kirk's desperate and insidious pledge and, to me, their inaction was downright shameful and dispassionate.

Even if I had gotten wind of it (which I didn't), I would have taken the initiative to check Kirk's assigned locker for some kind of weapon. After all, I was the person who officially gave out lockers.

However, the day went on, just like many other school days at our rather mundane and unheralded facility. I don't even recall a fight or a heated argument transpiring on the yesteryear day I'm remembering.

Seemingly, that symbolically was "the quiet before the storm." When the students were dismissed that afternoon, around three o'clock P.M., they noisily piled out of the building like they customarily did each weekday. And that included William Mason and Kirk Jones as well. Surrounded by a small cluster of teenaged classmates (girls and boys too) who were intent upon catching the local northbound bus, the two boys climbed aboard it also.

Of course, I wasn't on that bus (although I wish I had been), so I can't honestly report what took place on it as it followed its regular route. All I knew was it would, subsequently, be driven straightforward on an elongated road stretch and would often stop to pick up other northbound passengers.

But according to an adult rider who was aboard that fateful bus, a startled and horrified eyewitness, what did take place on that bus was surreal and almost unimaginable. The witness, a black woman who was en route to her workplace, reported that this young boy (later identified as Kirk Jones) was hurriedly trying to disembark the bus at the upcoming stop. She said he was "steadily" shouting out cuss words back at an older boy (who was William Mason) and, soon, descended the bus steps when it stopped. Then, the older boy walked up the aisle, with a bunch of other kids following behind him.

"And that's when it happened," that female eyewitness declared on the local news. "Before I knew it, I heard gunshots, a whole lots of them and I was scared for my life!" And that, in essence, was that. Kirk Jones had kept his desperate vow, a vow he had disclosed to a select audience of adults (mainly teachers). In broad daylight, with numerous people looking on, he murdered William "Billy" Mason, emptied his pistol into his victim, in fact. WHY? Because he had reached his absolute limit in being harassed, picked on and bullied. In a single and gruesome moment in time, Kirk Jones had snuffed out the life of Billy Mason and, in exchange, had sealed his own fate. Inevitable incarceration awaited a despondent and tormented teenaged black boy and there really was no exonerating rhyme or reason for it. Dr. Martin Luther King Jr., who, himself, was shot to death a few years prior, had once said, "Unearned suffering is redemptive," but it did not apply to the forestated case, not even for a grievous Kirk Jones.

In spite of not intimately or even casually knowing either one of the ill-fated young men involved in that shooting episode, I could not resist weeping for them in the short aftermath of it and, occasionally, I still mourn their tragic loss.

You may very well take exception to my lament, remind me that the Jones kid did not die in that horrific incident, but I thoroughly believe his spirit perished that day. And I doubt if it was revived or resurrected in a lonely prison cell somewhere.

Hopefully, you (the reader) are unable to relate to the foregoing and heartbreaking scenario of vengeful homicide. I honestly hope it's as foreign to you as a faraway region named "Timbuktu." Although it has always been far too common in the African-American community, no loving mother or father should ever have to contend with losing a child to an entity such as death or any form of extensive prison confinement either. And, sorrowfully, here, in the 21st century, my heartfelt wish is extended to the Caucasian populace as well.

For in the wake of multiple mass killings across our nation, it is crystal clear that bullets and bombs, both, are nondiscriminatory. And I only regret that that cannot be said about a multitude of fellow Americans. That, too, is shameful and grievous.

But in detailing my sad story about Billy and Kirk, there are valuable lessons to be learned. One of them certainly involves my teacher co-workers, and especially the select group who, apparently, ignored Kirk's cry for help. In reality, that kid was yelling, "Someone, please stop me!" However, I can't entirely omit my other work comrades either. Some of them had to see something or be aware of the ongoing conflict between those two boys.

Currently, I can't help but compare that yesteryear act of indecisiveness to the controversy surrounding the Ukraine "whistleblower," a courageous man or woman who a vindictive Donald Trump yearns to "out" him or her to the American public and, moreover, "tar and feather" her or him also. (At this point, I must pose a relevant question to you: What would that action do to other concerned citizens who become aware of blatant wrongdoing?).

Our nation's populace is frequently told, "If you see something (meaning, anything suspicious), then say something" and that cautionary suggestion was applicable generations ago also. As I stated before, I never personally witnessed the bad blood that existed between the two boys in action, but someone had to. And just because the observer's respective offsprings were not remotely involved in the matter, did not justifiably excuse their silence and inaction. After all, many of them were high school teachers.

There's, yet, another take-away regarding that long ago tragedy. It focuses on William Mason, the slain youngster. He was so intelligent and displayed so much academic potential that he had appeared on a local TV news program with our school's Principal and was verbally applauded for his superior test performances.

But, unfortunately, he wasn't smart enough or mature enough to realize that even iron shows signs of wear as time marches forward. Meaning, just because Kirk Jones had withstood his taunts and bullying for a lengthy period of time, didn't mean he would tolerate it forever.

Being the teenager whom he was, it was a fatal oversight on William Mason's part. Obviously, he was void of discernment and any degree of empathy. And that is almost commonplace with young people. Many of them are impulsive and somewhat self-centered too. If Billy had lived to reach adulthood, perhaps he would have cast off his bullying persona.

Unfortunately though, some individuals are career, unabashed serial bullies and Donald John Trump fits that profile like a well-tailored suit. It is his lifelong M.O. (mode of operation) and when one blends that outrageous trait with his well-entrenched sociopathic nature (which is actually inborn), it establishes him as "a clear and present danger" to our country at-large. As tragic as it was, young Billy Mason's bullying behavior, alternately, led to his fatal undoing, but I am awfully fearful that old Donald Trump's

"THE BULLY BEHIND THE PULPIT"

bullying tactics will, eventually, lead to our nation's undoing and I refuse to stay silent or lie dormant while that transpires.

Throughout Donald Trump's ongoing presidency, his political partisans, as well as his lockstep supporters (or base), have gone to great lengths to explain and attempt to legitimize the President's ugly and caustic words and actions. I've even heard a number of them casually dismiss his offensive conduct by replying, "That's just Trump being Trump" or "The President is a counterpuncher."

Well, throughout my long life I have occasionally dealt with a cluster of adults who, upon making a blunder or an ill-advised decision, choose to completely write it off by declaring, "That's just the way I am." And when I happen to hear such rationalization, and especially when it involves mistakenly or wrongfully hurting other people in some way or another, I not only believe an apology is very much appropriate, I cannot refrain from stating, "Well, that isn't the way you ought to be." Why is it so difficult or hard for some people to say "I'm sorry" or admit they have erred? Hopefully, one of Trump's avid confidants will one day summon up enough courage to pose such a question to his arrogant and shameless leader.

Of course, the foregoing is a hypothetical pipe dream on my part. Such a query will never, ever be asked by any Trump supporter because, in reality, they see him as I and millions of fellow Americans see him. They, too, are fully aware that the man is completely void of humility and human compassion and, therefore, he cannot bring himself to admit he is wrong about anything. They, his ardent loyalist, are cognizant that the POTUS has lived his entire life, basically self-absorbed with his own well-being and contemptuous of the plight of everyone else. And that, in a nutshell, is a concise description of the real Donald John Trump in living color.

Oh, by the way, do you recall how gracious and sincere the President was when he apologized regarding the Barack Obama "birther conspiracy?" Or when he conveyed his heartfelt regret for callously reducing brain concussions caused by warfare explosives to minor or mere headaches? Well, neither do I - because he never issued those apologies!

To be absolutely honest, there is nothing Donald John Trump says or does that surprises me in the least. However, whenever I hear one of his Republican colleagues rather proudly proclaim him as a "counterpuncher," I emerge intrigued in regards to the spokesperson's personal background and character. In reality, our President is a vindictive, thin-skinned, mean-spirited cry baby and blowhard and if an individual (any individual) can extract any degree of admiration from that on-target description, then he or she is deserving of a measure of serious scrutiny themselves.

If a single person applauds Trump's overt penchant for belittling and trampling over the feelings of other people (be they foe or a former friend), then that onlooking admirer is quite capable of doing the same, exact thing. And if, perchance, that is, indeed, your personal M.O., then I offer my sincere condolences to you.

Because if you happen to fit that mold, I am somewhat certain that you have wielded out plenty of grief and heartbreak during your ongoing life journey. I thoroughly believe that when a person comes to highly admire or esteem another human being, it's either because he or she aspires to be like the exalted individual or they, themselves, are already like the subject person. Deep in your heart, you can easily deduce if I'm referring to you or not. Hopefully, I'm not.

"THE EVIL THAT MEN DO"

Throughout my rather lengthy life, I have habitually advised people, and especially young people, that, "If you want others to say something good about you when you are nowhere around or are no longer in the realm of the living, then be of good cheer, treat all people decently and with respect and try to do good works."

But, to my utter regret, many people, including young folks, fail to heed or even consider my advice. For the most part, far too many people operate with a devil-may-care attitude and go through life, not overly concerned about people's opinions of them or their future legacy.

Well, if you live (or lived) alone on a distant island, I imagine that viewpoint would be understandable and somewhat moot. In addition, if you've gone through life, focusing solely on yourself and crying, "Hooray for me and the hell with everyone else," then that cavalier stance would surprise no one who truly knows you either.

However, if you have taken the time to love and befriend other human beings (whether they be relatives or otherwise), then it stands to reason that you'd take the initiative to provide those loved ones with a flood of wholesome and benevolent memories. And whether you're in town, out-of-town or in a casket or urn at life's end, then you should resign yourself to be a person who exudes fair play, congeniality and goodwill. And if you fit that stellar bill, and the majority of people in your social circle would prefer to see you "coming" than to see you "going," then your most intimate loved ones will celebrate the very day they first laid eyes on you.

Of course, I can't speak for others (and I admit to being an idealist and a sentimentalist as well), but I've always longed for my most prized loved ones to amass the same high regards and accolades I alluded to above. In fact, I've gone through life, desiring it for my parents, my brothers, my wife, my in-home and surrogate children, my relatives, as well as my diverse group of friends. And I'm quite certain that my cherished loved ones wish and desire the very same high regards for me.

Now, if you (the reader) have come to the conclusion that I've given out more advice than "Dear Abby" or "Ann Landers," then I would have to plead guilty as charged. But since I grew up, anxiously absorbing and, sometimes, clinging to the verbal wisdom coming from the mouths of a whole spectrum of mature and elderly Americans - I feel compelled, if not, obligated, to pass the baton on to future generations. Even as a child, I greatly believed in the premise, "With age comes wisdom" and I refuse to shirk my responsibility.

I also refuse to be like a passing ship in the night, an empty vessel whose chief concern is to stay adrift and aimlessly afloat. We, each of us, were put on this earth to make a significant and lasting impact and whether it's benevolent or adverse is, essentially, up to the individual. For you are the captain of that symbolic ship and if you elect to take on wandering passengers or not is solely up to you and whatever god you've come to worship.

As for me, I chose generations ago that I'd not only follow the path set forth by a man named "Jesus Christ," I would work diligently and tirelessly to persuade others, and especially children (mine, yours, everyone's children), to embark upon that same, less-travelled journey.

With that said, I would like to take a few minutes to reflect on a personal regret I've been made to bear, one that acutely applies to this particular soul-searching chapter.

My reflection focuses on my own biological father, Melvin V. Harris, and although some people might criticize or condemn me for depicting him in a negative and bad light (many of them, my beloved kinfolks), I speak of him in the name of my love and fond remembrance of him. Even in the light of a state of cessation known as "death," a man's voice can, sometimes, still be heard. But even more than that, a valuable lesson might be in the offing.

As I stated before, my dad was lauded as an extremely handsome black man. However, do not misconstrue my usage of the word "black." He showcased tan-colored skin, a head of ebony straight hair and sported an athletic build. In addition, he came across as well-spoken, debonair, suave and, seemingly, highly intelligent. In a certain sense, my father appeared to be too-good-to-be-true. And, to my great sorrow, my father was just that.

Behind closed doors, however, my dad was a virtual menace and terror, and especially when he was drinking alcohol (which was quite often). He was physically and mentally abusive to his wife and children and, in all honesty, that assertion applied to his first family as well as his second family.

Although me and my Saint Louis-bred brothers once jointly believed our father's tyranny was unique to our select household, we eventually came to realize that we were grossly in error. Whatever demons lurked inside of him (and, seemingly, there were many), they prevailed in the state of Missouri and followed him to neighboring Illinois too. Admittedly, I've gone through life, feeling, both, shame and sorrow for my dad. Not to beat a dead horse, but I still maintain that people basically never change.

In retrospect, my father spent a couple of years in the United States Army (a few years after I was born), and I credit him for being in my life for a mere nine years. Being the second son born into a family of five boys, there was a time when I adored my dad, when I wept heavily for him, even prayed for his departure and, strangest of all, deeply lamented not being my father's father.

From the time I was but eight years old, I frequently dreamed of being my dad's father wherein I would tightly embrace him, kiss his jaw and try to convince him that everything would turn out fine. Even in my immaturity, I felt my dad was "pissing" his life away and taking his good fortune for granted. To me, he was blessed by God to have a faithful and hard-working wife, he had a credible job (a public service bus driver) and he had five sons who were physically and mentally healthy.

But, apparently, there lied the main problem. In my child's mind, I viewed my father's circumstances as good fortune and an advantageous boost from the Supreme Being, while Dad appeared to perceive them as a curse and gut-punch, but not so much from an entity known as Satan, but from God, Himself.

Of course, I never knew if that even partially explained my father's disenchantment and disconnect with God, but it was certainly a pronounced truism. My dad held a life-long grudge towards the living God and it never seemed to dissolve or wane.

For example: When my dad died of cancer at the relatively young age of 50, I happened to be at the hospital, standing by his bedside. My father had but a couple of more days to live at that time but, in spite of being physically weak, he seemed to be in good spirits. In fact, he took the initiative to tell, both, me and my beloved half-brother (who was also present) in verbatim, "I love you."

That, to me, and my on-scene younger brother, was a Hallmark moment, a heartfelt declaration that touched both of our hearts. But not too long after that poignant scene took place, another memorable event transpired. However, it was completely void of warmth and any degree of human decency and compassion. Instead, it was abrasive and rather mean-spirited.

To be exact, my father was suffering from terminal esophagus cancer and, therefore, when he opted to express himself, he spoke in a very soft and raspy-like tone. But when a young Caucasian priest entered my dad's hospital room, holding an opened Bible, the old man's remark was somewhat loud, clear and quite nasty.

"Git the fuck out of here!" Dad angrily demanded. "I don't want you here!"

"THE EVIL THAT MEN DO"

Now, whether the clergyman was poised to share a comforting scripture with my father or deliver the last rites to him was anybody's guess. All I remember is the priest halted in his tracks, grimaced and soon vacated the room. I felt sorry for the befuddled clergyman and for my dad too, but I remained silent, hoping my father would not choose to pursue the matter. And he did not.

At this precise juncture, I feel compelled to cite one of my long-time pet peeves, but one that's quite compatible with my current commentary. In reading my book thus far, you might be well-aware that I have attended more than my fair share of funerals and memorial services during my lifetime. However, not because I'm mournful or macabre at heart, but essentially because those grievous ceremonies are actually for the on-hand mourners. In reality, I basically dread attending funerals (and regardless of my personal connection with the deceased person) and I oftentimes enter the church or mortuary, hoping the ceremony will not be overly long and not wildly dramatic.

But what irks me, what practically drives me up a wall is when I'm exposed to a blatantly false and undeserved, flowery eulogy. As I previously emphasized, "If a person wants others to speak well of him or her when they are nowhere around or deceased, then be a nice person and do good works."

I'm not advocating that the average individual should aspire to be a saint or even a true Christian, but, at least, try to be decent and treat others decently and, dare I say, "The way you wish to be treated."

And I am sad to divulge that my late father, whom I came to befriend and cherish as an adult man, did not remotely resemble the above profile. Therefore, in the midst of my Dad's funeral in 1975, when the residing minister commenced his eulogy by stating, "Melvin Harris found the Lord at an early age," he was, unknowingly, setting himself up for an instant punch line. Right on cue, as if it had been rehearsed, one of my younger brothers unashamedly inserted, "And lost Him soon afterwards."

UP-CLOSE AND PERSONAL

I, along with my four biological brothers, our half-brother and our stepmother were sitting together on the front pew at that time, and we collectively (essentially, the sons) laughed out loud. Seemingly, we couldn't help ourselves.

When the residing preacher went on to resume Dad's eulogy, I actually can't recall what else he said. Knowing me and my, sometimes, bizarre sense of humor, I very-well might have been thinking of the joke about a woman in the midst of an ongoing funeral service.

In it, the woman sat rather fidgety on a church pew, listening to a grossly prevaricated and complimentary verbal tribute (or eulogy) to the deceased person (a man who she well-knew as a scoundrel and a low-life), and wondered if she, indeed, was at the correct funeral. She was even tempted to approach the coffin and quickly peek inside of it.

As I pre-warned you, the foregoing was just a joke. But it's not so farfetched when it comes to a certain segment of people in our society. Those kind of individuals go through life, preoccupied with themselves and regarding all others as mere stepping-stones and bit-players in their self-concocted and distorted world.

Without any doubt in my mind whatsoever, our nation's current President, Donald John Trump, is a prototype of that unrelenting and diabolic philosophy. And with the Republican vanguard solidly in his back pocket, he is poised to take America to an all-time new low. Once again, I must say he's a career sociopath and demi-God who has no moral compass, no sense of right and wrong and will joyously sell his soul to the devil for a bargain price. And since he has no authentic love or allegiance to anyone except himself (not family, friend or political party), he is capable of bartering away our nation for little of nothing also. He enjoys playing the innocent and besieged victim, but, I implore you, please do not be duped or misled by him.

The man is shockingly aloof and totally unconcerned with the well-being of John Q. Public, and nor does he "honestly" concern himself with people's opinion of him. Beware the melodramatic hype! Trump is entirely incapable of acting presidential, but he's quite gifted at acting the brazen fool.

The title of this particular chapter is "The Evil That Men Do" and, admittedly, I took the liberty to borrow it from William Shakespeare's "Julius Caesar." In fact, it was spoken in homage to the slain Caesar and was concluded with "Lives after Them." However, when I focused my attention on our sitting President, I audaciously altered the words to, "The Evil That Men Do; Some Men Do Over and over and Over Again." And Donald Trump epitomizes my alteration.

I may come across as extremely cynical or unduly harsh and bitter, but unless Trump is subjected to some kind of life-changing event or religious epiphany, he will never alter his ways for the best.

General Douglas MacArthur once said, "Old soldiers never die; they just fade away." But when it comes to racist and mean-spirited government officials like Mr. Trump and Mitch McConnell, it should be asserted that, "Political partisans and pundits never die; they just nasty away."

And, please, don't misinterpret me. I do not wish for the sudden demises of neither the President nor Senator McConnell (God knows there are carbon copies of them eagerly waiting in the wings), because I personally sampled that unforgettable degree of grief and heartfelt sorrow when it came to President John F. Kennedy and Senator John McCain. Plus, I don't desire to be exposed to an orchestrated charade (a staged memorial service) whereby minion after minion comes forth and blatantly and unashamedly lies about a vindictive and unrepentant POTUS. Even his loyal base should not be made to endure such a contrived happening.

Is Donald John Trump a lost cause? Your guess is as good as mine. But, similar to my biological father, the man doesn't know God, he has zero interest in a Supreme Being and he behaves and operates accordingly. That is why, when someone (like Nancy

Pelosi), even suggests that they'll pray for him, Trump becomes totally unhinged. He can't remotely conceive of anyone (and especially a person whom he considers a political foe) praying on behalf of his well-being because he, himself, could never be that magnanimous. I'll say it once again, an inordinate number of people judge others by the way they, themselves, are.

No matter how many ministers or so-called Evangelicals opted to "lay hands" on the POTUS, I still maintain that the man does not have a religious bone in his whole body. His true God resides amidst money and power, always has. And that is why he was so disgusted and critical of Mitt Romney, a fellow Republican. When Senator Romney invoked his faith when he voted to impeach the President and have him removed from office (that was in February 2020), Trump was livid! Religious faith is as foreign to "the Donald" as the principles of integrity, righteousness and honesty.

There is nothing new under the sun regarding a faithless sociopath like our POTUS. Like a career criminal, his M.O. never, ever changes. When I use to hear people say (and thank God they've toned it down lately), "I wish he would "act" more Presidential, I always equated it with asking seasoned indecent individuals to act decent on occasion. I thought, "Hell - we once elected Ronald Reagan, he was a trained actor, but if you really want someone to act presidential, then you should have voted in accomplished thespians." People like Michael Douglas (he did well in "The American President") or Danny Glover (of the movie "2012") or even Morgan Freeman (he was a great POTUS in "Deep Impact"). Personally speaking, Mr. Freeman would get my vote hands down. After all, Morgan Freeman has not only portrayed a credible U.S. president in the movies, he played "God" in a couple of films too. You see, I do consider myself a person of faith and, therefore, I'm sure Trump would despise me too.

Now, I don't know if Donald Trump happened to see any of the movies I mentioned above (upon citing "2012" and "Deep

Impact," it would be like an American disaster watching a couple of disaster films), but it is more than evident that he's theatrical and melodramatic. But, in addition, it is also quite obvious that he solidly believes that there are select groups in our society who are uncaring, stupid, gullible and unbelievably naive as well.

In reflection, think back to the "State of the Union" address that Trump delivered on the evening of February 4, 2020. In my viewpoint, he was true-to-form when he, oftentimes, turned the address into a campaign rally (he even relished his Trumplican constituency shouting out "four more years"), but from the moment I heard him invoke the name "Dr. Martin Luther King Jr.," especially in a positive light, I knew something funny or out-of-kilter was coming up.

Before that address came to a controversial conclusion (which was when Nancy Pelosi tore up her copy of the speech), the POTUS had gone around the auditorium, shining a spotlight on a diverse group of African-Americans, all in a well-choreographed but rather shameful effort to garner black votes regarding the upcoming fall presidential contest.

Even in the middle of taking a prolonged victory lap on behalf of low black unemployment and an initiative for prison reform (he may, one day, break his arm from patting himself on the back), Trump cited a young, female African-American student who was in attendance; awarding her a scholarship. Then, he focused on a 100 year old black Tuskegee airman, granting him a military promotion and a stellar recognition too. And, in addition, the President took the initiative to shower Senator Tim Scott with a rousing round of applause and praise, who just so happened to be a loyal Republican (or Trumplican).

All of it was fashioned and tailored to appeal to easily-deceived and unsophisticated black voters and, sorrowfully, there are a number of them in this country. Unfortunately, many of my people are unaware of African-American heritage and social circumstances and, some, just don't give a rip.

But I mostly blame our white counterparts for that blatant oversight and disconnect. Black America is not cognizant of our history mainly because of white design and white power. Dare I say though? In three years' time we should be well-aware of Donald Trump's history and it's definitely not good. When he once asked, "What do you (meaning, African-Americans) have to lose?" I suggest that we immediately focus on the hundred or so conservative Federal judges he has appointed thus far. In my estimation, "conservative" is a code word for racist. I ask you, "What are they trying to conserve?" Please, wake up and smell the coffee, my black brothers and sisters!

However, after all of Donald Trump's fake and disingenuous posturing during the State of the Union presentation, whereby he strategically wooed and elicited the black vote, Trump could not refrain from being, well, Donald Trump. Just like the dairy cow who yielded a full pail of milk and, then, kicked it over with his hind foot, he boldly went on to award controversial radio personality Rush Limbaugh the 'Medal of Freedom.' Even in his superficial and cellophane attempt to tone down his racist nature, his greater demons grinningly stepped forward.

But I astutely saw through that pandering maneuver too. Sure, Limbaugh was reportedly struggling with stage-4 cancer (but so was Congressman John Lewis, a black civil rights leader who walked proudly with Dr. King), but it didn't alter the President's biased and conservative agenda.

Rush Limbaugh has always been just as racist, misogynistic, crude and mean-spirited as Donald John Trump. They both hate former black President Barack Obama with a passion and, in fact, were staunch proponents of the now-debunked "birther conspiracy." Therefore, when the POTUS announced the recipient of that prestigious medal (which was previously awarded to distinguished individuals such as Martin Luther King Jr., John Steinbeck, Rosa Parks and Neil Armstrong), he killed two birds with one stone.

"THE EVIL THAT MEN DO"

In Trump's calculating and devious mind, he felt confident he had fooled a number of "dumb and ignorant Negroes" and, simultaneously, had pleased his racist base by celebrating the abrasive ideology of one of their very own. And make no mistake about it. That obscene stunt appealed to Neo-Nazis and white supremacist too.

Oh, and by the way, if you think Rush Limbaugh and Donald Trump are not "Birds of a Feather," then I suggest that you review film footage of the POTUS mocking a physically-challenged man during one of his rallies, as well as Limbaugh's visualized effort to poke fun at 'Michael J. Fox' as the actor dealt with body tremors which were derivative of his Parkinson's disease. I also remember that despicable man (Limbaugh, of course) calling 'Chelsea Clinton' a "dog" when she was but a young, innocent child! Maybe you (as a reader of this book) are able to dismiss nasty rhetoric as normal and tepid, but I consider it awful and blatantly evil. What if he said it about your child? And I'd like for you to mull over this query also: Would our President and his wife, Melania, take exception to someone making such a demeaning remark about their young son? In Trump's outrage and ever-present vindictiveness, he'd be tweeting his butt off!

"IN PURSUIT OF COMPASSION AND EMPATHY"

"IN MY LIFE - THERE's been heartache and pain." Upon citing that declaration, I was not feeling sorry for myself or lamenting my past life. I'm just quoting a line from one of my favorite songs. The song is entitled, 'I want to know What Love Is' and it was performed by a group called "Foreigner."

In my personal opinion, the lyrics to that tune captures the authentic gist of the human experience. Meaning, I believe that in the midst of heartache and pain, human-kind is continually in search of unconditional love and affection. And that quest is not restricted to only romantic love either. It includes love of God, love of parents, love of siblings, *bromantic* and *sismantic* love (or friendship), love of children (but not only yours, all children) and a demonstrative love for mankind in general.

I know I'm a dreamer, and I admit to being a creature of imagination too. But, upon looking back at my life and savoring all the beautiful memories that helped to define my very being, I cannot refrain from wishing that others (and especially individuals who exude compassion and heartfelt empathy) would incur and enjoy life-journeys similar to mine.

However, even when I reference my foregoing life and my, somewhat, philosophical blueprint for serenity and lasting joy, I'm acutely aware that familiar adages such as "Different folks, different strokes" and "You can't paint all people with the same broad brush" stands in the shadows to take issue with me.

"IN PURSUIT OF COMPASSION AND EMPATHY"

Akin to a foregoing saying I invoked, which was "One man's junk is another man's treasure," I'm fully aware that our personal pleasures (or treasures) are diverse and subjective also. In addition to saints and true-Christians, unfortunately, sociopathic, sadistic and masochistic people dwell amongst us too. So, I get it, we are all very different.

However, not to distance myself or catapult myself above other people, but I've spent my whole lifetime trying to spread joy and good cheer to others, and especially to children and elderly citizens. Personality traits such as selfishness, self-gratification and self-absorption have always been secondary, if not, nonexistent, to me and, to be frank, I have felt this way since my early childhood.

But guess what? Although I'm certain that some folks will charge me with "tooting my own horn," but I'm essentially unmindful of that criticism. I realize that my personal M.O., or thought-pattern defies the so called 'norm.' It is rather weird and unorthodox, even to me, I'm not ashamed of my innermost feelings. Instead, I am quite proud of them.

Admittedly, from the time I viewed two unrelated Hollywood movies, I knew I was quite different from a lot of people I interacted with. In Cecil B. DeMille's "The Ten Commandments," wherein Moses saved an elderly slave woman from being crushed to death, I felt emboldened by Joshua's subsequent words. The biblical Joshua, a Hebrew slave himself, struck an Egyptian overseer in his efforts to rescue the woman in peril. And minutes later when Moses asked Joshua, being well-aware that the heroic slave faced his own execution for striking the overseer, "Who is the old woman to you?" I was instantly touched.

Without any hesitation at all, Joshua responded, "An old woman."

Now, I didn't know how any of the other kids in that theatre felt upon hearing Joshua's reply; not my brothers, not a one of them, but I was impressed and heartened. It messaged to me that one does not have to be blood-related to be afforded another individual's compassion and concern.

Then, shortly after seeing DeMille's epic production, I was exposed to George Steven's western film entitled "Shane," Just so happened, I had read the novel, but even if I hadn't, it was easy to tell that Shane and Marian were attracted to each other (even Joe, Marian's husband, was aware of it) and they, both, the woman and Shane were respectful of the marriage vows.

As the story progressed, right after the ferocious fight between Joe Sr. and Shane, wherein Shane, alternately, rendered Joe Starrett unconscious by hitting him with the butt of his pistol, Shane was preparing to ride into town and reckon with the villainous bad guys. It was then that Marian softly asked Shane, "Are you doing this for me?"

And without little thought on his part, Shane (similar to Joshua in DeMille's movie) sincerely stated, "For you, Joe and little Joe."

Once again, I didn't know about other people in that theatre, not my mother, who was sitting next to me, or anyone else, but I felt exhilarated and warm inside. I previously acknowledged I've always been emotional so I, too, was weeping, just like the kid named 'Joey,' when Shane rode off into the night.

But, at the end of that classic western, Joey still had a father, but I didn't. My dad had already disappeared from my life and even if he had been still around, he could not have held a candle to Shane's exemplary character and scruples. Even in those yesteryear days, I wished my assessment was wrong. If you recall, I had observed my father's behavior with other women.

Throughout my life, I confess to having an ongoing love affair with the cinema. In some ways, movies have helped to shape my character and morals as well. But, in other ways, they have validated my inborn thought-patterns. Even when my father was still on the home-front, I held precise views of right and wrong and justice.

For instance, my mother treated me to "Gone with the Wind"

"IN PURSUIT OF COMPASSION AND EMPATHY"

when my dad was still on the scene, years before I was made aware of Dad's womanizing. Without anyone saying anything to me (neither an adult nor a fellow child), I entertained definitive views regarding marital fidelity.

Therefore, when the film went on to depict Scarlett O'Hara's unabashed lust for Ashley Wilkes (even after he spurned her and, then, married another woman), I was in awe and befuddled too. Even as a little boy, I branded Scarlett as conniving, shameless and evil.

In fact, after viewing the entire movie (and it was a long one), I came away, silently applauding and admiring only three different characters from the laid out storyline. I esteemed Rhett Butler for his valor, his unpretentiousness and decency; I liked Melanie Wilkes for her pardoning and gentle nature; and (although it was a rather demeaning role) I loved Hattie McDaniel's portrayal of "Mammy." Being a young African-American myself, I was proud of her irrepressible ethics and sense of morality.

In essence, I grieved on behalf of Rhett's long suffering but unrequited love for Scarlett; I was impressed by Melanie's forgiving and loving spirit when it came to Scarlett's overt dallying with her husband, Ashley; and I felt like giving Mammy a standing ovation when she subtlety chastised an overbearing Scarlett, reminding her that Ashley was wedded to Melanie. I relished Mammy stating, "He's her husband, ain't he?"

Most certainly, movies are basically made for their entertaining value. But many of them are message-oriented and tend to linger in people's minds well-after the theatre's lights are turned on. Speaking for myself, I attend movies, hoping to learn something new or be exposed to a different perspective on a myriad of issues. And, sometimes, when I find myself virtually overwhelmed by the toils and worries of life itself, seeing a single movie lifts up my morale and sagging spirits. And, upon being frank, for the last three years, I have seen a ton of movies.

However, well-before I became preoccupied with the

continuous antics and reckless and lawless behavior of President Donald John Trump, I enjoyed my life to the very hilt. And most of it, I'm happy to report, involved a great deal of movie-going too.

As you (the reader) surely knows at this particular juncture, I am a senior American black man. I have always been relatively poor, but a formidable battler when it came to life's assorted woes and challenges. Totally unlike our divisive and godless POTUS, who was born into unearned wealth, I have spent most of my life, trying to be Christian-like and, in close concert, to bring a measure of joy, enlightenment and sunshine into the lives of everyone I've had the blessed fortune to interact with, and especially children.

On that additive, I have a rather strange-and bizarre confession to make (strange to you, maybe, but not to me). When I physically see or mentally reflect on individuals I've come to dearly love and cherish, I visualize their "child-hood" face and demeanor. Admittedly, I cannot adequately explain it but it is a lifelong phenomenon I've been made to contend with.

Whether people buy into it or not (and I certainly would not fault them for it if they do not), but when I'm in the company of a person whom I knew and loved when he or she was a child, I visually see the former child, not the current adult. And, in addition, when I entertain fond thoughts of them, the same phenomenon occurs.

For example, over the years I have immensely enjoyed seeing and conversing with the only Caucasian "true-friend" I've ever had. We are both 75 years old at this time and, at 18 and 19, we served together in the United States Army. His name is "Tommy" and he's been to Saint Louis several times and I've vacationed in San Antonio, Texas (where he currently resides) a number of times as well. And, yet, when I have the chance to see him in person and take the time to talk to him on the phone, I see the smiling facade of the eighteen year old teenager whom I originally fell in love with in the early 1960's.

As I confessed, I agree it is weird and hard to fathom (maybe,

"IN PURSUIT OF COMPASSION AND EMPATHY"

my father knocked a screw loose in my brain during one of his beating episodes), but it has become something I greatly relish and regard as a unique blessing.

Now, I wish I could claim that my life has been "a bed of roses" or something even remotely resembling that wonderful and envious description, but I cannot honestly make such a statement. Maybe, there are a few citizens in our country who could 'rightly' describe their life as a virtual bed of roses (after all, there are exceptions to every rule), but I can almost guarantee you that the boasters of that 'flowery' claim would be white and not black, and especially before sporadic school shootings came to the national forefront.

Prior to the onset of that tragic and violent-prone era, it seemed that the black community had a iron-glad lock on gun-violence and acts of lethal savagery. And although Caucasian people, in general, appeared to be unconcerned and, somewhat, oblivious to the ongoing bloody carnage in America's inner-cities, I, as a seasoned black man, derived no pleasure or satisfaction upon watching random school shootings that rocked the very foundation of white communities.

Quite the contrary, I wept heavily and grieved for all of the murdered, wounded and forever-traumatized Caucasian kids involved. Because they, in fact, were precious children, as well as living and breathing human beings. I saw devastated, innocent kids and their skin color was totally immaterial and a non-factor to me. That's what true empathy and compassion is all about.

Even in my old age, I still dream of the futuristic day when the greater majority of our white brothers and sisters can actually see beyond skin pigmentation, when they can fully accept religious differences and sexual orientations too. However, I won't hold my breath. As yesteryear actor, John Wayne, stated on the silver screen and long-ago singer, Buddy Holly, expressed in a popular song, which was, "That'll be the day, I remain skeptical."

However, please don't get me wrong! I'm not insinuating or denying that there's not an inordinate amount of killings and criminal activity that plague America's black community. I credit a great deal of it to abject poverty, absentee fathers and a well-entrenched but overlooked disease called, self-loathing amongst our own ranks.

But to be perfectly honest, I have personally known and, in select cases, loved individuals who murdered fellow black people, some - who were murdered themselves and, yes, several young blacks who opted to murder themselves; people who were evidently so despondent and desperate that they chose to commit suicide.

Even as I continually grieve on behalf of that latter group (although I still lament the others too), I regret not being on hand to assure each of them that a better and brighter day was on the horizon.

And "we" (people who are of a compassionate and loving nature) must assure our present day children, and especially the vulnerable ones who are now fostering the belief that the world would be a better place without them in it, that they cannot dissolve a temporary problem by resorting to a permanent solution such as self-destruction. And I implore you (the reader) to seriously mull over the following: Over the years, I have known and have read about a number of so-labelled "gay" individuals who, tragically, elected to take their own lives. But, I can't help wishing that they could have, somehow, remained steadfast and/or co-existed to be privy to the current and contemporary era, wherein the average person is more tolerant and less judgmental than foregoing generations. In my estimation, this particular day happens to be the select day that, both, John Wayne and Buddy Holly alluded to so many, many years ago.

However, before I proceed further, I feel compelled to share one more tidbit of heartfelt information with you, but one that's acutely related to the forestated commentary. I've always pinpointed it as my self-concocted 'litmus test.' Upon conversing with parents who happened to rather ashamedly admit that they were contending

"IN PURSUIT OF COMPASSION AND EMPATHY"

with homosexual offsprings (and there were more than just a few), I emerged with the same, straightforward verbal advice.

In earnest, I wasn't being flip or disingenuous (I could actually feel their pain), but I would softly ask them, "Would you rather have your gay son or daughter emerge from a previously closed closet or see them lying in a state of repose in a coffin, with their secret well-intact?" And, in some cases, it is just that simple and cut-and-dry. Naturally, I cannot speak for you or anyone else, but, as for me, I would choose the former hands-down every time.

At this precise point, I can imagine people asking me, if they could: "Since you priorly acknowledged that you do not have any biological children of your own, why do assorted parents seemingly solicit your advice or opinions in regards to young people in general?"

Believe it or not, I view that as a fair question and I'll try to be equally as fair upon trying to address it. Anyone who has known me through the years, anyone, would tell you that I have an insatiable love for children, all children.

In addition, many of those same people are well-aware that I worked in a number of inner-city high schools for several decades (three of them, to be precise) and I closely bonded with a whole spectrum of upstanding and respectful teenagers along the way; some of them, black, some, who were white, and a couple who just happened to be of Asian descent.

Notably, most of them worked for me as 'student helpers' (for a modest salary), broke bread with me as cherished surrogate children, attended assorted movies and sports events with me and, one of them (who was Vietnamese), even resided with me and my family for a year or so. And without any reservation whatsoever, I dearly loved each of them (still do).

However, I am not naive, gullible or easily duped when it comes to people in general. Therefore, not to sound like a broken record (Late in life, when I drove a school bus, a teenager asked me, "What's a record?"), but I still maintain that the average person sizes-up and judges others by the way they, themselves, are. So, in spite of being (to some degree) admired by a number of onlooking people for my rather uncommon track-record with a diverse group of children (and in spite of how long they've known me), I'm not so sure that all of them assess me at face-value.

In essence, since a segment of those observers cannot picture themselves in my shoes, then maybe my actions and associations with unrelated youngsters are suspect and, even worse, devious to them. Plus, although no one has ever opted to express it to me, I imagine, too, that a select few felt that they are "normal" and I, on the other hand, am not.

Believe me, I am not being paranoid or over-analyzing the matter, it's just that I'm acutely aware of the biasness and foibles of everyday people. Much of the time, people are all over the map with their self-deduced assessments reference any matter. However, in reality, I cannot control anyone's innermost feelings about anything, except my own.

In a manner of speaking, I am not what the average man or woman considers "normal." And they might, very well, be right on the money about their assessment. Since I've never been quite sure of what normal really is (and I've admitted that before), I am obliged to plead "guilty as charged." Therefore, due to the fact that I'm much too old to change boats in the middle of a stream, I have no other recourse but - to say "I've Gotta Be Me."

In my personal viewpoint, there is nothing mysterious or remotely bizarre about my intense love for children (nor for people in general, for that matter). Goes without saying, my feelings can be traced directly back to my somewhat gloomy, relatively poor and strife-filled childhood. Owing to my father's erratic and brutal conduct in those early days, I vividly recall the heartfelt anguish and tear-streaked faces of my quartet of brothers, along with the assorted bruises that were sustained by our victimized mother. Those are the scars in my mind that have tremendous staying power and seem totally immune to healing.

"IN PURSUIT OF COMPASSION AND EMPATHY"

What I recall mostly in those days was being worried, angry, anguished and indescribably sad. Stands to reason that I seldomly smiled in the midst of a single man's repetitious tyranny (who, of course, was my own dad) and I also painfully remember that frequent deficiency also.

Now, I know it's ironic, but when I mentally reflect on my overt affection for kids (again, all of them), I cannot avoid thinking of my father. For certain, the man can be indirectly credited for a sizable portion of my affirmed and resilient love for children (although, not at all intentionally), but, contrarily, that's not what prompts me to focus on him. As odd as it might seem, it boils down to a vocalized advertisement from yesteryears.

When the old man was still in the family photograph, he habitually smoked 'Camel' cigarettes (which, probably, led to his rather early demise) and that brand of 'smokes' had a popular slogan, one which was often broadcast on the radio and the television as well. Till this very day, I have never smoked anything (not even a marijuana joint), but, nevertheless, I grew fond of the words in that slogan and even mimicked them on occasion. Furthermore, as the years went by, I took the liberty to revise them, projecting my own, heartfelt feelings.

The original slogan stated, "I'd walk a mile for a mild, mild Camel." However, my homespun version declared, "I'd walk a mile for a smile on the face of a single, precious child." And that, in a simple nutshell, captures the main thrust of my entire life and being.

To my utter regret, I was never adequately equipped with the tools or resources needed to enhance the lives of all children (a tool such as money) but I was blessed enough to extend a measure of sunshine and priceless time to a select few of them. And their individual smiles and faces of sheer joy remain forever etched into my brain and memory bank.

In retrospect, I was married for 28 years and had it not been for the pervasive breast cancer that, alternately, took my wife's life in

July of 2007, I am quite certain that she and I would still be wedded today, here in 2020. However, I didn't recite the matrimonial vows until I was at the ripe old age of 35. My rather late blooming could not have been attributed to some kind of anti-marriage stance (although my mother's two marriages were totally disastrous) or a lustful desire to be a roving playboy. Simply stated, it was because I hadn't met the "right" woman at some point and I was extremely happy and content before I met the "right" woman as well.

There was a time when I was deeply in love with a young lady, a lady who was formerly married and just happened to have three children also; but, unfortunately, she did not love me back. However, I wasn't totally disheartened. Apparently, she "liked and respected" me and I still loved her. Within the framework of the well-known adage, "Hope springs eternal," I kept the love-light burning for quite a spell.

But there was another development that arose in the relationship, one that tended to baffle onlooking people, but, actually, seemed natural and appropriate to me. Even as my romantic craving for the young lady gradually waned, I thoroughly grew to love and cherish her three young offsprings; two boys and a girl.

I didn't care if I wasn't biologically connected to her kids and I wasn't remotely deterred by the fact that they weren't my responsibility either (a thought that was voiced by a few 'buttinskis' in my life), I just out-and-out loved them! I loved conversing and interacting with them, I loved hugging and consoling them and, more than anything else, I loved seeing them smile and in a state of happiness and contentment. All of that, to a man of sentiment such as I am, was purely magical, almost heavenly!

However, I admit to being somewhat of a hoarder when it comes to people I dearly love. Therefore, the special bond I forged with the sibling trio, did not, in any way, offset, impair or negate the close-knit relationships I enjoyed with other assorted young people. If you recall, I pre-stated that I adored all children.

"IN PURSUIT OF COMPASSION AND EMPATHY"

So, in having a beloved Godson, an array of nieces and nephews, young prized cousins and a group of surrogate sons whom I met and bonded with during my lengthy work tenure with the St. Louis Public Schools, I engaged in a rather elaborate juggling act. With little thought on my part, I indiscriminately meshed our ongoing lives together. And, oftentimes, we (the assembled group) entertained only three pertinent questions: Where are we going? When are we going? And - How are we going to get there?

Of course, I was instrumental in answering the latter query. Being the single adult involved, my personal automobile was mostly our source of travel regarding our ventures. In addition, I frequently pinpointed the specific time when we'd engage in the various outings or affairs. And I feel compelled to state the following: Every young person who was privy to my social circle and respective plans, fully knew my word was my bond. Their anticipation was my aspiration.

However, I wasn't the sole decider of our varied destinations for fun and enjoyment. It certainly wouldn't shock anyone when I declare that "we" (myself and a diverse mixture of my youthful cohorts) pilgrimaged to a vast number of movie theatres that were located in and around the city and counties of St. Louis, Missouri. Within those venues, we enjoyed such films as *"The Poseidon Adventure," "Guess Who's Coming To Dinner?," "The Towering Inferno," "It's A Mad, Mad, Mad World," "Goldfinger,"* "To Sir, With Love," both, *"God-father 1"* and *'Godfather 2," "Star Wars," "A Soldier's Story," "Walking Tall," "Dirty Harry,"* assorted westerns and comedies, and so many *"Dracula"* features that starred actor Christopher Lee, it would make the average person's head spin.

But theatre-going, while extremely popular with the majority of our group, was not the only pastime we engaged in. We also spent time at the "Ringling-Brothers Circus," the "Shrine Circus," "Six Flags over Mid-America," the "Royal American Carnival," the "Forest Park Zoo," "St. Louis Cardinal baseball games" and even a "Harlem Globetrotter exhibition." And, not to minimize its worth, but many of the forestated outings (and especially the movie-viewing) were capped off with a dining episode at a popular Saint Louis restaurant. Notably, I hardly ever dined inside a restaurant when I was a kid.

Now, although none of the youngsters I associated with were aware of it, I never particularly relished outdoor activities. (Truthfully, I dreaded being in a mobile field hospital when I was in the army). I never cared for picnics, lawn parties, boating excursions or, significantly, fishing. I made it a point to say "significantly" because the two male siblings (the boys I alluded to a while back) seemingly loved "fishing." And I truly loved seeing them fish. It was always a Kodak moment to me. Therefore, my suppressed distaste for outdoor activities was entirely vanquished by the glowing smiles on the faces of those two brothers. That, too, was pure magic to me.

In reality, it wasn't a great sacrifice for me, my personal knack for extracting a feeling of delight and warmth from observing a loved one engaged in an activity that I secretly disliked. I wholeheartedly bought into a particular line from a long-ago song entitled "Downtown" and it, to me, sealed the deal. That memorable lyric was, "You must realize that it's all compromise" and I've always held firm to that wise rationale. (Hell - throughout my enduring marriage I didn't mind accompanying my wife to a 'Tupperware Party'). In essence, if I "survived" a ballet with you, then you should be able to "tolerate" a baseball game with me. Some individuals might deem it, "Tit for tat," but I regard it as plain-old fair play.

To be totally transparent, the foregoing commentary was more geared to my philosophical views regarding a successful marital union than an enticement to continue to peruse my close-knit and intimate relationships with a diverse group of children. I saw a relevance in the assertion and I opted to expound on it.

Upon returning to my foregoing life before taking the marriage plunge in 1979, it is noteworthy to report that my ongoing

"IN PURSUIT OF COMPASSION AND EMPATHY"

interactions with a hodgepodge of kids, especially teenagers, was not restricted only to the Saint Louis area. Throughout the years, I frequently took Gus and Tony to Chicago, Illinois (those were the brother duo's names), but mostly during the weekends. And there, I (more or less) managed to kill two birds with one stone.

My father had passed away in 1975, but my kid-brother and my stepmother still resided in Chi-town and me and my two surrogate sons relished visiting them. And to my utter delight and heartfelt appreciation, not one time did the boy's mother object to my taking them out of town. Therefore, she might not have loved me in the manner I wished she did, but apparently she trusted me.

However, I had a burning desire to widen the horizons for those two boys, and I was almost obsessed with it. A close male co-worker and I had driven to Los Angeles, California during the summer of 1972, I thoroughly enjoyed cross-country driving and I virtually loved the scenery that comprised that road-trip. Therefore, since I had managed to amass five thousand dollars by 1976 (which was a minor miracle in itself), I set the wheels in motion for a lavish, carefree, three-week "dream" vacation in L.A.

To be completely honest, I had affixed my mind to that fantasy trip several years prior, actually in the short aftermath of my initial trek to 'The City of Angels,' so there was nothing remotely "spur-of-the-moment" about it. On the contrary, it was well-planned and well-anticipated.

To be precise, I had a relatively-new hatchback automobile (a Pontiac Ventura, to be exact), I had a comprehensive road-service agreement, I had pre-booked our hotel lodging at a 'Ramada Inn' in Los Angeles, I had thirty-five hundred dollars in traveler's checks and fifteen hundred dollars in cash, and the Triple AAA Automotive Club had expertly mapped out the impending driving route.

Although the lyrics which were outlined in Nat King Cole's famed "Route 66" song were almost true to perfection (which was considered 'the southern route'), we were also poised to stop at the

"Painted Desert" and the "Petrified Forest" and, in reality, that did come into fruition.

Although it was also my intent to take 'the northern route' back to St. Louis (wherein we'd visit the 'Grand Canyon'), that particular idea died on the vine. In spite of having ample funds left (I still had nine hundred dollars to my name when we embarked upon the return trek), I reluctantly shelved that phase of my plan, favoring a more expedient return to Missouri. Although I lived to regret not overruling my three-child traveling entourage, I had grown somewhat weary of hearing them individually ask, "When are we going to get there?" So, since the southern route happened to be shorter in distance than the alternate route, I made the decision to retrace our former steps on our return destination.

Admittedly, it wasn't a "typo" or a lapse of memory on my part when I referred to "my three-child entourage" above. That's because the brother pair was not exclusive to my well-crafted vacation plan. As I divulged earlier, I had a cherished Godson named Patrick or PJ (who was my best friend's eight year old son) and that little boy, too, was an intimate part of our pre-slated, cross-country journey. And although PJ was somewhat junior to the teenaged brother-duo, he was a compatible fit in my opinion. I loved him from the day he came into the world and the brothers seemed to like him also.

In looking back, I am happy to report that that vacation, in itself, was virtually everything I had hoped (or dreamed) it would be. At the motel, the three boys had access to the on premise swimming pool, thanks to a diverse group of popular restaurants, we ate all three meals out, we spent days on end at renown and well-advertised pleasure sites such as "Disneyland," (two days), "Magic Mountain," "Knottsberry Farm," the "Hollywood Wax Museum," "Universal Studio" and even the "Farmer's Market." In addition, when we weren't enjoying any of the pre-named attractions, we could often be found at one of L.A.'s inexhaustible

"IN PURSUIT OF COMPASSION AND EMPATHY"

movie complexes. And since I also had a number of relatives and a few friends who resided in the Los Angeles area, we were almost always on the move. Therefore, I, along with my three young charges, were all-smiles throughout that entire journey and absolutely no degree of boredom or disenchantment was ever our nemesis. Personally speaking, it was a dream-come-true and the marked happiness on the faces of the boys involved remain forever etched into my mind. I only wish that everyone, especially families, could be exposed to similar lifetime memories. For to me, it was positively and unequivocally beautiful! I thanked God for keeping us safe during that lengthy road-trip and for the utter joy He so graciously extended to us.

However, it may surprise or even shock some of the readers of my book, but the foregoing vacation experience did not fully sate my appetite for bringing a novel joy to young people or my penchant for travelling across the country. In 1978, just two years after that Los Angeles extravaganza, I made provisions to embark on, yet, another long automobile trip. But instead of California or anywhere near it, I selected Orlando, Florida which was the home of, both, "Disney World" and "Sea World."

From the very onset of that particular dream, it was already my desire to include the same three boys who accompanied me to L.A. in 1976. The respective parents involved were quite susceptible to my plan and even kicked in two hundred dollars.

Now, if it sounds to you like the "same soup warmed over again," then your assumption would be grossly in error. It was because, in regards to the 1978 trip, I elected to add two girls to our Florida trip. One girl was the younger sister of the brother pair (Debbie) and the other young lady (her name was Tracy) was the daughter of the school's secretary where I worked at that time.

But to my undisclosed regret, that travel venture was not as well-planned as the foregoing one. Since I had only saved thirty-five hundred dollars for that trip (the extra two hundred dollars helped) and I was obliged to pre-book and pay for two different

UP-CLOSE AND PERSONAL

rooms daily (it was a 'Quality Inn' and the rooms were adjoined), I was financially challenged from day number one.

Similar to the L.A. trip, the six of us ate every meal out, we went to such renowned places such as "Disney World," "The Wax Museum," "Sea World" and the likes and we were privy to many motel amenities, which included the on premise swimming pool. In addition, our group, too, was in the vicinity of numerous movie theatres.

Here, in the year 2020, I still find myself marveling over the smiles and vast expressions of delight that appeared on the faces of my five travelling companions in 1978. That adventure was also memorable and magical to me. My only regret was that I ran short of money and, therefore, wasn't able to stay in Orlando for as long as I wished.

To be completely candid, I had exactly five dollars to my name when I arrived back in Saint Louis proper. (No one could ever convince me that God does not exist!). However, in spite of the depleted funds issue, that Florida trek, just like the preceding pilgrimage to California, was absolutely wonderful and I enjoyed them both to the very hilt.

As I acknowledged before, I didn't get married until I was 35 years old. That was in December of 1979, approximately seventeen months after the trip to Orlando, Florida. I dearly loved my wife and her 12 year old biological son as well, but my overt affection for children in general never subsided or waned. My wife was totally aware of my feelings and they never became a divisive or difficult topic. All I knew was that I had, yet, another child in my life to spoil and cherish (my beloved stepson) and that was more than fine with me.

But, on a few occasions, I did apprise my spouse that I was happy even "before" I took my marital vows. Now, upon admitting that I voiced that declaration to my wife from time to time, I can imagine some people saying, "You are strange, weird and rather stupid too!" But I am not at all dumb or a glutton

"IN PURSUIT OF COMPASSION AND EMPATHY"

for punishment. When I opted to tell her I was happy prior to getting married, I made it my strict business to quickly add, "But since I married you, Honey, I have been positively ecstatic. You see, my mother didn't raise no zip damn fools! I knew how the game was played.

"CHRISTIANS, EVANGELICALS AND DEVILS"

"I'M A 21 YEAR OLD CAUCASIAN MAN WITH BLOND HAIR AND BLUE EYES."

ADMITTEDLY, THAT'S A DECLARATION THAT'S not only a gross exaggeration, it's an out-and-out lie! And it definitely is not wishful or envy-driven thinking on my part. As I stated in the previous chapter, "I've Gotta Be Me." And I must also add, I like being me.

I opened this chapter with that absurd falsehood because I wanted to make a comparative point. I could make claim to being a young "blond-haired, blue-eyed white man" a thousand times daily but, in real time, I'd still be the same seventy-plus African-American man I am proud to be. Therefore, the foregoing declaration is essentially nil and void.

However, it directly leads me to my relevant point. Throughout my life, I have interacted with numerous people who truly consider themselves "Christians." Not aspiring Christians, but bonafide Christians! To be more precise, a large number of people obviously deem themselves Christians solely because they emphatically and unequivocally say they are.

"CHRISTIANS, EVANGELICALS AND DEVILS"

Well, excuse me for pushing the "spoiler alert" button, but their bold pronouncement does not necessarily make it a done deal. They may attend church services every Sunday, they (or you) may be faithful in paying their tithes and some might even be on the usher board or sing in the church choir, but if their hearts are not right, then they are just slapping their gums together when they declare, "I'm a Christian."

Oh, I can imagine the outrage permeating from many people who read my foregoing comments, especially the ones who solidly perceive themselves as Christians. And, please, do not confuse me with a person who feels "holier than thou," because you will be totally off the mark.

Although I do aspire to be Christian-like, I do not identify myself as a true Christian. But guess what? I do know one when I see one. And, thus far, being on the cusp of turning 76 years old, I am sad to say I have rarely seen one.

That is the meat of my rather provocative argument. Anyone with a vocal cord can insist that he or she is a Christian, but at the end of the day - what does that mean?

I have known many young men who begrudged and brooded over their absentee fathers and, from time-to-time, I have tried to serve as a stand-in dad, a mentor or a role model to some of those youngsters. But along the way, I have diplomatically (not dogmatically, mind you) recommended the Holy Bible to them. Not because I'm some kind of religious fanatic, but because of a figure called "Jesus Christ" I found inside of it.

And I did say "figure" because I'd tell those young men that, "Even if Jesus is not (or, was not) the true son of God, He (the man himself) is a person to admire, emulate and aspire to be. Even if Jesus died on the cross in vain, his relatively brief existence on earth is something to applaud and appreciate and marvel at. So, in spite of my being in the lives of many of those select young men, and even if they are never again associated with another tangible and flesh and blood role model, they could actually familiarize themselves with such a stellar figure by studying and reading about Jesus Christ in the Holy Bible.

Maybe, Jesus didn't feed the multitude of people with a few fish and loaves, maybe, He didn't turn water into wine or even cure people of a variety of physical and mental maladies as well, and, maybe too, He didn't really raise Lazarus from the dead, but He (or he) led a commendable, exemplary and admirable life.

Regardless of the actual number of people involved, Jesus did feed the hungry, He ministered to the sick and disabled, He preached hope and salvation to the forlorn and downhearted and, most certainly, He is (and has always been) an everlasting model for compassion, empathy, self-sacrifice and heartfelt benevolence. And whether we visualize Jesus Christ as a black man, a white man or whatever, He epitomizes and personifies "unconditional love" and "selfless goodwill" like no other figure in the history of the world.

Personally speaking, I have always been totally fascinated with the well-documented life of Jesus Christ. I even set my sights on trying to be "like" Him. But I, just like any other human being with such an illustrious ambition, has stumbled from time to time. However, even in my failings, just like writer and poetizer Maya Angelou famously stated, "Still I rise."

I remain steadfast in living in the glowing shadow of Jesus Christ and I try to encourage others, and especially children I was blessed to know, to do likewise. More than likely, they, too, will fall somewhat short of that aspiration but, still, I beseech them to try to emulate and follow the teachings of Jesus Christ.

And I tell those kids something else also, something that enhances their individual lives for many years in their future. In spite of their chronological ages, I implore them to be keenly discerning when it comes to everyone they meet - and look long and hard for Jesus in the hearts of those select people as well.

Plainly stated, I encourage young men and young women to

"CHRISTIANS, EVANGELICALS AND DEVILS"

make it a point to seek out "goodness" and "moral virtue" in all people, whether they be adults or fellow young people. And if it appears that those special qualities are practically nonexistent in the subject person, then I suggest that one should limit his or her association with the individual involved.

Am I suggesting that people (especially followers of Christ) be "discriminating" regarding other people? Emphatically - YES! But it has absolutely nothing to do with religion, sexual-orientation, skin-color or any other surface feature. If you happen to believe that Jesus is, indeed, the son of the living God (as I do), then it stands to reason that you believe that God truly exists too. And if that is correct, then it's also logical to believe in a foreboding entity known as "Satan" as well. And although millions of people will vehemently criticize my reasoning and audacity, that brings us to a despicable human being named Donald John Trump, our country's sitting chief executive.

I'm not accusing the American POTUS of being the devil Himself or the foretold biblical "Antichrist" either (in my opinion, Trump is not that clever, persuasive or powerful), but I do see the evil that resides inside of him and numerous tell-tale signs of his unholy alliance with Lucifer, the devil. And I saw it and perceived it from day number one, when he stooped to capture dramatic impact by ascending that escalator (pretending to be God on High) and, alternately, announced his candidacy for president of the United States.

While a multitude of people seem to be totally unphased by the scandalous, bizarre and vindictive behavior of the current President (especially his loyal and fanatical base), I continue to see him as a clear and present danger to America and, maybe, to the world at-large.

Although his staunch supporters and political pundits traditionally stand ready to make a variation of excuses for Trump's blunders and unorthodox behavior, their assertions are mostly false, superficial and rather juvenile. Shamelessly, they mouth everything from "He's a counterpuncher," "That's Trump just being Trump" to "Oh, he was just joking." But the bottom line is, both, simple and academic. Although many people casually dismiss it as frivolous and beside the point, Donald Trump definitely is not a nice man. And while the average person will go to great lengths to avoid caustic and mean-spirited individuals in everyday life (such as co-workers, neighbors, relatives, etc.), it boggles the senses to acknowledge that millions of American citizens rousingly applaud and, oftentimes, exalts a President who consistently displays so many grotesque and unsavory character traits.

And although Trump's followers are quite adept at citing the economy, employment surges, tax breaks and the stock market as his stellar accomplishments and claims to fame, it doesn't excuse the man for being essentially void of common decency and any semblance of compassionate feelings for other people. And if you are amongst those who see Trump as a champion and a man of integrity and admiration, then you are probably cut from the same soiled cloth.

And, notably, since the forestated accomplishments I alluded to came to light later on in the Trump presidency and his hideous conduct was well-publicized and very much on display prior to him taking the oath of office, it suffices to conclude that there was another force or lure that drew steadfast loyalist to the Trump camp. And although many of those ironclad supporters will squeal like a hog with a dagger stuck in its side when I express this, I thoroughly maintain that their overt attraction to Trump is adorned and embroidered in racial hatred. Well before he launched his presidential bid, people were generally apprised of Donald Trump's racist history and agenda.

Many of those people (even the ones who chose and still choose to wear blinders) were fully aware that Trump's own father was a classic racist. And it is said that, "When you see the son, then you see the father." And many of those same people were cognizant of the President's blood-thirsty bigotry regarding the so-called

"Central Park Five." But even if they were entirely ignorant of both of the forestated factors, unless they lived on an alternate planet, they surely were knowledgeable that our current POTUS was a die-hard promoter of the "birther movement." And since a large segment of those observers were "Barack Obama haters" themselves, that fabricated narrative endeared them to Trump even more.

During Hillary Clinton's run against Trump, she branded his base "*deplorables*," but I perceived her criticism as somewhat harsh and superficial too. And I'm prepared to tell you why.

Although we, as human beings, traditionally regard other people as "basically good," I'm afraid that's a false perception. Truly "good" people (like authentic Christians) are at a real premium in this world. Even before the "Me Too" premise came to the American forefront, we were already entrenched in and driven by the "Me Only" mind-set. Unfortunately, the majority of the populace in this world (and not just our nation) are concerned and obsessed with "self" and, maybe, a few individuals in their immediate families and social circle.

And that, in a tidy package, summarizes why so "many" people (not all of them) admire, esteem and, almost, fanatically support Donald Trump in practically anything and everything he either says or does. Down deep, there are numerous supporters who march lock step behind the POTUS simply because they, themselves, are exactly like him.

For example, if they could bring themselves to denounce or chide Donald Trump's racist and biased character, then they, in essence, would be criticizing their own embedded bigotry and ideology and they are not about to do such a thing.

However, my personal bone of contention goes far beyond my accusing a large segment of Trumpers being racist and hate-mongers themselves. That's a done deal, in my opinion, and I leave their fate in the hands of God. But, it continues to vex and baffle me when so many Americans, regardless of their gender or racial origins, pretend or persistently argue that the final verdict is still out when it comes to our President being a racist at all!

Most certainly, it is not politically prudent or expedient for a Caucasian candidate to be considered a bigot or a racist in 2020 America, and especially when a President is seeking a second term. But, in the spirit of a frequently echoed rationale, I am almost compelled to say, "If it has a hard bill, then it's a duck. If it has webbed feet, it's a duck. And, if it quacks like a duck, then it is a duck." (And, in this particular case - a DONALD DUCK).

Now, I have long-believed that the 'his' in the word history is a pronoun that essentially substitutes for "white." Therefore, it simply translates to the "white (man's) story." Traditional American history books details and, oftentimes, sanitizes the deeds, exploits and actions of the Caucasian race from the moment they set foot on North American soil. In addition, I took the initiative to study the plight of black Americans in this country also. So, I am keenly aware of what African-Americans have encountered, endured and have suffered through since they were forcibly "brought" to the shores of America as well.

Therefore, I am "unshockable" and somewhat "immune" to an age-old scourge and fully metastasized cancer that's famously known as "racism." And in my honest but depressing opinion, it will never wane, let alone perish altogether. I pray that I'm wrong or, to some degree, mistaken, but I surmise that there's an inordinate number of die-hard Caucasian citizens who feel emboldened and superior by despising and looking down upon people of color. And I further feel that that ilk of people will die out well-before the death of overt racial hatred.

Although there is no way to deduce any degree of justification from the Caucasian race's historical and ever-present desire to suppress and devalue the worth of other races of people (and not only the African-American race), I am fully aware of their mind-set. There's nothing new under the sun regarding their cravings.

Rev. Dr. Martin Luther King Jr. preached a sermon in the

"CHRISTIANS, EVANGELICALS AND DEVILS"

1960's entitled the "Drum Major Instinct" and its contents hit the proverbial nail on the head. It indicated that almost universally people (in general) covet and dream of being the select individual marching out front, leading a gala parade. But Dr. King didn't stop there. Instead, he went on to point out that "races" (especially, the white race) and even nations (especially, the United States) are obsessed with the same elitist yearning and maintained, too, that they would stop at nothing to realize their ambition.

I choose not to reiterate the reverend's common sense viewpoint he so aptly stressed in his sermon, but when he summed it all up, urging individuals to aspire to be "first" and "foremost" in qualities such as 'compassion,' generosity,' 'love' and 'charity,' it exemplified his powerful message. He emphasized that even everyday people can achieve a measure of greatness and prominence just by committing their lives to any one (or all) of the forestated qualities. In that vein of thought, everyone and anyone could encompass a degree of greatness, he advocated.

As I stated above, I elect not to review Dr. King's yesteryear sermon at length, but I am hopeful that people will one day take the time to seek it out. I found it tremendously uplifting, inspiring and teeming with logic.

But to be honest, when my mind seriously revisits Reverend Dr. King's "Drum Major Instinct" sermon, it presents me with an alternate insight and rationale - when it comes to the Caucasian race. If Dr. King's take on that cited 'instinct' (or impulse) is, indeed, right on the money (and I am thoroughly convinced it is), I can see why "racism" is so entrenched, beloved and favored by a large margin of white citizens in this nation. And with that said, it also explains to me why there are so many white people who refuse to admit that the American President is a homespun racist. Their admission would severely taint and cripple Trump's assumed feeling of greatness as well as theirs.

I've said it before and I'll say it once again: "Nothing white people do (and, sadly, I'm referring to the overwhelming majority of them) remotely surprises me." Now, I know that particular declaration reeks of stark pessimism, but over the years I've been obliged to hope for the very best, but expect the very worst. So, when Trump surrogates audaciously attempt to disassociate the POTUS from his racist nature, I instantly stash their efforts in file 13. And I see them for who they really are; phony and disingenuous puppets.

Being in my mid-seventies, I am well-aware that people, in general, are very different. As of late, people on television (especially on news programs and specifically black citizens) almost constantly retreat to the phrase, "Black people are not 'monolithic,' meaning that African-Americans are not all alike. And I heartily agree with that common sense remark. It's a declaration that's applicable to every race on the face of the earth.

However, when I hear a fellow African-American alibiing and trying to make a case that Donald John Trump is not a bigot or a racist, I am amazed and beside myself with wonder and subdued anger! Even if the black spokesman (or spokeswoman) was unaware, or totally dismissive, of the President's bigoted father or Trump's personal blood-lust when it came to the "Central Park Five," as well as his sick and perverse jealousy and hatred of America's only black POTUS, the subject spokesperson had to be knowledgeable of the man's racist conduct and agenda after reciting the oath of office.

The African-American spokesperson (no matter who they were, where they were or when it was) had to be aware of the President calling black football players "sons-of-bitches" (and also yearning for them to be 'fired'). They knew he gave the green light to biased police officers to "play rough" whenever they actively arrest black suspects (in spite of their guilt or innocence). They were cognizant of Trump labelling predominantly black regions "shit-hole countries," even while touting the "white" populace of Norway as the ideal and preferred immigrants to come to the shores of America.

"CHRISTIANS, EVANGELICALS AND DEVILS"

And, furthermore, I'd venture to say that those subject spokespersons were not ignorant to him calling 'White Supremacist,' the "Ku Klux Klan' and 'Neo-Nazis' good people also. In addition, those black Trump defenders knew that our Chief Executive, similar to talk-radio personality, Rush Limbaugh, was a strong proponent of the infamous "birther movement" and they positively knew (or now know) that he audaciously awarded his staunch confederate, Mr. Limbaugh, the distinguished 'Medal of Freedom.'

And, lastly, but not to be overlooked, while the President was engaged in a decriminalization initiative that was designed to provide a sense of justice and fair play to black folks when it comes to incarceration (Trump even pardoned a select number of African-Americans), he turned right around and methodically installed nearly 100 so-called "conservative" judges to the federal bench.

Conservative, to me, has always been a watered-down synonym for "racist." Therefore, the long-standing turnstile for black imprisonment will continue to revolve around and around. And I must add this: I have never had any idea of what conservatives are hell-bent on conserving. Maybe, one of these days they'll apprise me of what it is. However, with the rapid rise of the Trumplican Party, I can make an educated guess in regards to it.

But, in the meantime, I am still somewhat puzzled and intrigued as to why American citizens who resemble me (meaning, black folks) do not see the POTUS as the racist (or white nationalist) he actually is. I realize that "money talks" and, unfortunately, millions of people (race, notwithstanding) will sell their soul to the devil for the right price. And Donald Trump, just in being himself, is well-attuned to that premise. So, although I cannot justly fault black "Trumpers" for their mercenary conduct and actions (I'm not cognizant of their personal circumstances), I can't bring myself to denounce or condemn them entirely.

But what about well-known African-American individuals like 'Kanye West,' a person who's not remotely hurting financially?

What about blacks who are pro-white? What about African-Americans who are self-loathing, the ones who have no compassion for people who resemble them? And - What about light-skinned black people who detest dark-skinned blacks, or vice-versa?

The foregoing sounds kind of silly and ridiculous, does it not? I totally agree! My people (black people) are not 'monolithic' but, for the most part, we are all mixed up - not physically but mentally. WHY? Because we were an enslaved and severely mistreated race of people and are, basically, ignorant of our history and heritage.

And I hate to admit it, but a select few of us are so screwed up mentally, Donald John Trump could shave his head clean, dress himself in a Ku Klux Klan outfit and gently put a noose around our necks and we'd still insist that he's not racist!

Although you (the reader) might find my latter assertion somewhat amusing, I am markedly serious about black people in America being mentally mixed up (not mentally ill, mind you) but the underlying blame cannot be solely attributed to us. I am sure I'll raise the dander of millions of our Caucasian brethren, but unequivocally the lion's share of the blame has always been in their biased and suppressive camp.

Earlier in this book, I conveyed that I worked as a 'Book clerk-Treasurer' for the Saint Louis Public Schools, and exclusively in an array of high schools. In that position (which lasted over three decades), I had the responsibility of ordering and distributing "approved" textbooks to the teen-aged students who were enrolled there. And I pursued my job with diligence and pride.

In addition, I familiarized myself with every book and pamphlet in the secondary curriculum and that included various novels and novelettes that were made available in on premise school libraries as well.

Therefore, in the early 1970's when the Board of Education installed a brand new Superintendent (who was white, of course), I was alarmed and appalled by a sudden, audacious and, in my opinion, nefarious alteration. It may surprise many people, but

"CHRISTIANS, EVANGELICALS AND DEVILS"

when I started working for the Board in 1968 (only 6 months after Dr. King was assassinated), there was a textbook entitled, "Eyewitness: The Negro in American History." It was a relatively thick book (maybe, three or four hundred pages) and it had a red and black cover.

Well, with no warning whatsoever or even a superficial reason as to why, that aforementioned textbook, along with assorted black novels such as Ralph Ellison's 'Invisible Man,' Martin Luther King's novels 'Why We Can't Wait' and 'Where Do We Go From Here?,' Richard Wright's 'Native Son,' Maya Angelou's 'I Know Why The Caged Bird Sings,' James Baldwin's 'The Fire Next Time' and even Alex Haley's 'The Autobiography Of Malcolm X' was completely removed from the approved curriculum list.

With the swift wave of the age-old racist wand, those books systematically disappeared from shelves. During the eighteen hundreds and well-prior, it was against the law to teach black people how to read and, in the nineteen hundreds, racist forces prevailed to try and diminish African-American books we desired to read.

However, here, in the 21st century, the average black citizen is free to read and mentally digest all the literature and books they choose to. And it's imperative (if not, essential) to encourage our black children to engage themselves in the same, enlightening task. And if our kids don't read about anything else, we, as loving and caring adults, must make a concerted effort to urge them to at least read about the black man's well-underplayed role in American history.

It's a fascinating read, something to actually marvel at and I truly believe it can be a far-reaching game-changer. I am thoroughly convinced that if young black people are honestly apprised of our plight, our remarkable resilience and the numerous contributions we allotted to this country, they will emerge more tolerant, more compassionate and much more loving also to fellow black people. And that's an inspiring goal that's well-worth striving and fighting for.

Now, I can hardly expect you, the reader, to remember this: But when I embarked upon this particular chapter, I made a personal admission and I was being totally frank about it. I stated that, "I aspire to be 'Christian-like' but I don't identify myself as a "true Christian." Although I didn't take the time to highlight or point it out, I just finished explaining why I have come to believe that "authentic" (or true) Christianity is beyond my personal reach.

Over the years, I have become somewhat of an expert when it comes to the horrific and unprecedented grief and suffering of black-skinned people on American soil. Therefore, I am acutely aware of the age-old pangs of slavery; the brutality, the dehumanizing, the alienation, the disenfranchising and the blanketed suppression of the human spirit. Rev. Dr. Martin Luther King Jr. aptly cited it as, "Man's inhumanity to man" and centuries of barbaric slavery was surely that and much, much more.

In addition, I am well-attuned to hundreds of years of lynching's, racial terrorizing and random murders, a home-spun pox called 'Jim-Crow,' deeply-entrenched segregation, housing and voter suppression and blatant institutional racism. As I previously indicated, absolutely nothing surprises me in white America. But I can't help stating this: I oftentime emerge shocked and somewhat taken aback when I'm exposed to literature or documents that even suggests that many of the prime perpetrators of the specified inhumane atrocities and acts of savagery dared to regard themselves as "Christians." Hell, even the Ku Klux Klan considered themselves a Christian organization!

However, even as I deem my recent declaration as the epitome of hypocrisy and, then, toss it into file 13, I still want to reflect on (what I perceive) as a personal religious flaw, the one factor that keeps me at bay from realizing true Christianity. Throughout my lengthy life, I have more than familiarized myself with the past and current misdeeds or sins of the collective Caucasian race. I

"CHRISTIANS, EVANGELICALS AND DEVILS"

explicitly and painstakingly divulged my overall knowledge of white history.

After many, many years of extensive praying and thinking and rethinking, I eventually arrived at a comfort zone wherein I could co-exist and forgive (but not remotely 'forget') the whole of the Caucasian race for the greater majority of atrocities and inhuman aggression they orchestrated and levelled on the black race throughout known history.

And for an individual who has always regarded racism as totally illogical, stupid, devil-inspired and a form of mental illness as well (meaning myself, of course), the calm and strife-free consensus that prevailed on me was rather miraculous in itself. There was a time in my life when I practically loathed the Caucasian race!

However, since I dreamed and aspired to be a Christian, I realized that "hate" was completely contrary to the teachings of Jesus Christ. Therefore, I denounced hatred and chose 'love' instead, and with the affection and support of a few "good" and "faithful" white comrades (especially, my lifelong friend, Tommy), my former feeling of loathing and disdain has gradually dissolved.

But steadfast "forgiveness" is very much in the Christianity equation also. And although I recently declared that I forgive our white brothers and sisters for their yesteryear (and current) racist sins and actions, I admit to falling somewhat short in one, specific area. While forgiveness resides in my heart for every other infraction and indiscretion (despite the severity), I constantly struggle with trying to forgive them for tampering with and distorting the mind-set and psyche of so many African-Americans. And I'll make my argument in the upcoming chapter. It's a forgiveness factor that I long to someday overcome.

"UP CLOSE AND PERSONAL"

During 2020's 'Black History Month' (February), my 17 year old grandson came to me, asking, "Grandpa, did you see the movie 'Birth of a Nation?" I answered "Yes" and my young questioner proceeded to reflect on the film's basic plot-line, letting me know he was aware of what it was. He said it was about Nat Turner's ill-fated slave rebellion in early 1800's America.

In actuality, I was glad he had seen it (motion pictures such as 'Selma,' Malcolm X,' 'Amistad,' 'Glory' and Alex Haley's 'Roots' saga are, both, educational and insightful to black folks), but after telling him that I was unhappy with the selected title of that film, I took the initiative to specifically explain why. To me, it was a teachable moment.

I informed my grandson of D.W. Griffith's 'Birth of a Nation,' which was a 1900's silent film that not only glorified and exalted the rise and savagery of the Ku Klux Klan, it visually dehumanized people of color and, more significantly, served as a well-tuned vehicle to promote and justify relentless murder, tyranny and racial genocide. And since my grandchild had never heard of that original, despicable and awful movie (let alone, see it), I expounded on its intent and all-too-obvious message.

After assuring my grandson that white actors, doused in black paint, were the on-screen players in that film, I also told him that white women were depicted as "virtuous" and as "pure" as the driven snow; so pure, in fact, that they would choose to kill themselves rather than be ravished and raped by barbaric and sex-crazed ex-slaves or so-called African-American 'freemen.'

And that, of course (according to the subject film and the white man's post-slavery mind-set), was the black man's obsession when human bondage (hundreds of years of slavery) was finally rendered unlawful in America. In essence, even though black males knew they'd be subsequently lynched, brutally tortured and murdered and, frequently, be disemboweled if they actually satisfied their sexual cravings, they went full-speed ahead anyhow.

Therefore, allegedly African-American men were not only incapable of denouncing and controlling their overt sexual drive when it came to those "virtuous" white females, they were foolhardy, callously stupid and self-destructive as well. Now, I can't speak for fellow black Americans (my people), but I've always found the foregoing rather hard to believe! To me, it is incomprehensible.

However, within the framework of my 'teachable moment,' I also told my grandson that that silent film was shown across America and in the White House itself shortly after its release. And, furthermore, I urged him to seriously mull over a certain underlying factor. Because I've been in my grandson's life since the day he was born, he is well-aware of my ongoing love affair with movies in general. In fact, I've personally treated him to an undeterminable number of films; everything from 'SpongeBob Square-Pants' to 'Toy Story' to the 'Muppets' to, and including, Marvel's 'Avengers: End Game' and several 'Spiderman' features.

So, when I pointed out to him that literally thousands (if not, millions) of impressionable Caucasian kids and adults, too, were introduced to that turn-of-the-century very graphic and controversial movie, I, then, encouraged my grandson to mentally reflect on the farreaching impact (meaning, the looming future) it might have had on the psyche of all yesteryear white youngsters, some who were, probably, his current age. More or less, I was urging him to employ a measure of critical thinking to the matter.

Personally speaking, I have always regarded the silent production of 'Birth of a Nation' as a racist-inspired "teachable hour or two," as well as a vulgar visual tool for unadulterated white hatred and violence. Reference my beloved grandson, I viewed it as 'food for discerning thought.'

Frankly, it has never been my intent or desire to teach any black child, including my teenaged grandson, to hate or be specifically begrudging towards the Caucasian race. Throughout history, our white brethren have waged unrelenting horror and tyranny on people of color, but I choose to leave their impending fate and comeuppance to the Supreme Being.

But, admittedly, I have always sought the answer to a relevant and exceedingly logical question. "Why is it that people, regardless of their race, creed or religion, teach their children and intimate loved ones to hate and denounce select fellow human beings, fully aware that their extreme biased feelings may, someday, cause their loved ones retaliatory harm?"

For instance: Although this may come across as somewhat simplistic and trivial, but when I was 12 years old and a 5 year old little white boy casually said, "Hi, nigger," I was instantly ticked off. In fact, if that kid had been my age or even my size, I would have tried to knock his teeth out. I had a trigger temper in those days and, in the throes of desegregation, I had been "called out of my name" several times by white boys before. Unfortunately, a fistfight accented those occasions and all because of the "N-word."

Therefore, my anger wasn't novel when it came to that 5 year old Caucasian boy. Here was a kid who lived in an affluent neighborhood and was a member of a very well-to-do family also. And since the 'nigger' term was hardly ever (if ever) spoken on network television in those days, where did he pick up on it? Some intimate grown-up, more than likely his dad or mom, used it quite often in his presence.

So, this is my common sense rationale: If you're not going to be around your child 24-7 and, therefore, not in the immediate vicinity to protect him or her during times of strife or conflict, why do so-called parents think nothing of jeopardizing their offspring's well-being or safety by mentally arming them with incendiary and provocative character flaws?

I don't care how tough or able-bodied you think your respective offsprings are (they may be as powerful and fit as a premiere bodybuilder), but there's always someone waiting in the wings who's tougher and more determined and, on occasion, more desperate. In your heart, you may be well-aware that you raised and nurtured an out-and-out bully, but he or she is not invulnerable. I suggest you re-read my chapter entitled "The Bully behind the Pulpit," wherein I disclosed the ill-fated story of 'Kirk Jones' and his nemesis, 'Billy Mason.' Billy was the aggressor in that tale and Kirk was somewhat smaller, but the latter kid resorted to a pistol as an equalizer.

So, again I ask, "Why do some parents or guardians implant seeds of hatred and discord in the hearts and minds of their children, rather than a quality that'll enhance their life, such as love?" I've always longed to hear a sensible and logical answer to that particular query.

And since I'm currently on the questionnaire circuit, and I made reference to 'bullying' as well, I wish someone, anybody (whether they be a staunch ally, a die-hard Republican or a qualified psychiatrist) would tell me why they are fascinated with or attracted to Donald John Trump? In other words, and I'm not being bitter or begrudging when I pose this query, but in spite of the envious lure of Trump's reported wealth or his current presidential position, why would anyone (man, woman or child) truly desire to be in the man's immediate presence?

Firstly, it is indisputable that he's a chronic, pathological liar and, apparently, he cannot help himself. ("I'm the least racist person you'll ever know."). Secondly, he's a classic narcissist who suffers from delusions of grandeur, and fully expects people (and especially his political minions) to lavishly praise and bow down to him. ("I know more than the generals."). Thirdly, he's a notorious and absurd braggart, a man who falsely perceives himself as an expert on anything and everything under the sun. ("Like a miracle, the plague will soon disappear.").

Fourthly, he's an ill-informed, semi-illiterate and self-promoting dummy; an individual who, obviously, has read only 'The Art of the Deal' and, maybe, 'Fun with Dick and Jane.' ("I'm a stable genius."). Fifthly, Trump's a strong and, almost, fanatical proponent of overt and undying loyalty (to him), but, evidently, sidesteps that quality when it pertains to himself. ("I don't know Michael Cohen."). Sixthly, he's a well-known womanizer and philanderer (who is void of morals and scruples), but hypocritically thinks absolutely nothing of chiding and denouncing other men for their personal indiscretions. ("I grab 'em by their pussies."). Seventh, he is shamelessly vindictive and verbally abusive to any and every person who opposes or even slightly disagrees with him and, obviously is barren of any degree of sympathy or forgiveness. ("Lock her up!" or "He's probably looking up" (from hell).

And, finally (although I could go on and on and on about Trump's deep-seated flaws and vices), and without any semblance of doubt, he is, both, faithless and is plainly (as I previously stated) not a nice person.

However, if you happen to be one of the individuals who finds this President charming, interesting, charismatic or socially tolerable (and there are millions who apparently do - his rousing base), then I suggest that you entertain a relevant question before you actually mingle with the man in the future. You must ask yourself, "Which butt-cheek would he prefer I kiss first, the left one or the one on the right?" Oh, and, please, don't forget to bow several times before your self-proclaimed king.

Of course, personally I look forward to 'never' meeting Donald John Trump or anyone who's like him. And I wish many fellow African-Americans were not acquainted with the man either, and especially individuals who behave foolishly or come across as mentally defected in his presence. Such as the black man who was on-hand when the POTUS hosted a disingenuous 'Black

History' affair back in February of 2020. Although the black spokesman was off-camera, he yelled to Trump, "You're the first black president!" In the short aftermath of that absurd and bizarre shout, the President sat, grinning like the fabled 'Cheshire cat.' For he knew, if he couldn't count on a single black vote for his fall reelection contest, that outrageous shouter was squarely in his corner. I don't know for sure, but when Trump once deemed a supporter "My African-American," maybe he was the man who yelled out that remark.

Naturally, I was momentarily upset and taken aback when I heard such stupidity spilling from the mouth of a fellow black man. It was a devil-inspired insult to all African-Americans who are aware of our former and on-going struggle for freedom and survival in America, and it was especially disparaging of our esteemed and former black president, Barack Obama.

But, to my heartfelt sorrow, I wasn't remotely surprised by that boisterous outcry. As I said before, it would not shock me to see a black man proudly wearing a KKK robe.

As I also priorly stated (in the foregoing chapter, in fact), "I constantly struggle with trying to forgive them (meaning, Caucasians in general) for tampering with and distorting the mind-set and psyche of so many African-Americans."

However, in spite of my lengthy and continuous struggle, it is tragically depressing and disheartening to acknowledge that a large segment of black Americans apparently fell prey to that age-old conditioning. And to my personal sorrow and utter regret, I have known and interacted with far too many of them. And although several of my long-time comrades deem it as a unique blessing, my personal 'vividness' (or total recall) regarding those rather sickening interactions, it is a nagging burden I'd like to cast off. Hopefully, upon sharing a few of them with you (the readers), it will serve to lighten my load somewhat. That 'select' few of them are as follows:

Case No. 1 In the year 1958, I entered high school as a freshman. That was somewhat of a milestone for me and I relished it. In addition, in that same year, I happened to meet the first African-American man (along with his immediate family) who hailed from the so-called 'Deep South;' Mississippi, to be specific. His family was comprised of a wife and three young children, all girls.

While visiting my mother (my mom was actually a close friend of the man's older sister-in-law), I was on hand to hear the man relay an interesting, but almost unbelievable story. As if it was normal and commonplace (and, maybe, in the south it was), he said he had been a long-time sharecropper "back home." Being a city boy myself, I was vaguely aware of what 'sharecropping' entailed but when our guest went on to divulge that he was being paid a meager $900.00 a year, I was momentarily speechless and flabbergasted as well! However, the man vocalized that remark in such a matter-of-factly way, I elected to remain silent.

Although I didn't say it out loud, I knew that man could easily improve his life and thrive financially in St. Louis, Missouri and, in my estimation, in any other state not located in the south. And I was remarkably right in my assessment. In two months' time, the man from Mississippi was working at a well-known automobile assembly plant. And not only that, he was allowed to work substantial overtime hours also. So, suddenly, like a dream come true, the man was earning an excess of $950.00 bi-weekly!

In my opinion, it was "too much, too soon" for him, something akin to culture shock. Within six months, he bought himself a shiny new Cadillac, two or three colorful suits, a wide-brimmed black hat and established a bold, indiscreet love-liaison with a homely looking white woman. Then, not too long afterwards, he broke up with his black wife.

More or less, my mother was attempting to put the entire happening into perspective when she posed a certain question to me. She asked me, "Can you imagine earning a lousy nine hundred dollars a year and then, all of a sudden, you're making almost two thousand dollars a month?" My mother was always quite witty, so

"UP CLOSE AND PERSONAL"

what she said next did not surprise me in the least. She reasoned, "No wonder that boy went hog-wild and pig-crazy! He couldn't help himself."

Case No. 2 When I was a 17 year old high school student, I lived quite a distance from my assigned school and, therefore, I, sometimes (when I could afford it), rode a public service 'streetcar' to my academic destination. I was sitting up front, minding my own business, when a middle-aged black woman climbed aboard the trolley and I happened to observe her when she handed the 'Caucasian' conductor a one dollar bill. The driver gave her proper change and all of that was standard operational procedure, no big deal.

Then, since I was seated alone in my seat, the same woman, displaying a very pronounced grin, casually took the initiative to sit down next to me. That, too, was copacetic. But, upon seating herself, the woman elected to loudly and almost excitedly apprise me of the origin of her wide smile. She began by asking me, *"Did you see that, young man?'* White folks - they are so darn smart! I gave him a dollar bill, and he already had my change in his hand! They be thinking' while we be sleep. I'll tell ya - they are so darn smart and intelligent too!"

While surrounding passengers mildly laughed (most of them, fellow Negroes), I wasn't even slightly amused. In fact, I was somewhat miffed. "Ma'am, do you see that sign up there?" I spoke, simultaneously pointing at a printed notice on the streetcar's front window. "It says, 'We accept and break one dollar bills only!' White people aren't so smart, but some black folks are really very stupid!"

"Aw, you're one of those nasty-ass nigga boys," the woman angrily responded. "I wish I wouldn't have even talked to you at all!"

I sat, shaking my head in subdued disgust and quietude. However, I couldn't avoid replying, "Yeah, I wish the very same thing, Miss."

Case No. 3 When school "desegregation" prevailed in Saint

Louis in the mid 1950's, I originally thought it was a 'good' thing. I knew it would be a lot of hostility and friction between the races but, for the most part, I hoped it would gradually and eventually bring us together as a free nation. Little did I know, however, that a select group of fellow African-Americans would emerge as "pro-white" and "anti-black"

Such was the case when I became acquainted with an obese, dark-completed and braggadocious African-American high school teacher named "Andy." Andy was a middle-aged veteran teacher and was well-known by his educational cohorts, and especially the Caucasian ones. In fact, that group practically loved him and oftentimes lavished him with joyful praise. However, their spirited accolades were vexing and somewhat shameful to me (and to quite a few other black staff members also).

To be specific, despite being a tenured teacher, Andy was heralded for being a no-nonsense, strict disciplinarian, which, notably, was not a part of his job description. But to the delight of his white colleagues, his self-imposed disciplinary actions were applicable to only black students, and certainly not the Caucasian ones.

Frequently, you would hear white faculty members around the school mouthing such words as, "Go get big Andy, he knows how to deal with 'um" or "Andy doesn't take no guff or bull crap from 'um, none of 'um." And, of course, the 'um in those declarations exclusively referred to black students (and, mostly, the males).

So, in a nutshell, those white teachers were stating, "If you are made to contend with a difficult, insolent or defiant black boy, then send for Andy and he will immediately straighten the damn kid out."

And what did 'straightening out' a black male student mean to 'good ole boy' Andy? Or to his on-hand, encouraging white comrades? Oftentimes, it meant bluntly punching the obstinate young man in his gut or chest area and, sometimes, knocking him to the floor. And when it came to Andy, there was no hesitation and no discussion whatsoever as to the reason why. As far as the burly and headstrong enforcer was concerned, the one-sided scenario of the involved white protagonist was adequate enough.

Andy's eventual downfall transpired quite abruptly and expediently one day. On that particular afternoon, after confronting, yet, another defiant black male student, Andy proceeded to deliver one of his patented right hooks to the boy's chest area, but, simultaneously, the youngster tried to dodge the blow by awkwardly ducking away. However, that evasive action didn't work out for the boy or his attacker. As the boy whimpered and writhed in severe pain, his adult brutalizer had mistakenly struck him in the facial area and had actually broken his jaw bone.

In the short aftermath of that shameful episode, the police and an ambulance was summoned and they, both, arrived on the scene. The young man, of course, was transported to the nearest hospital and Andy was promptly arrested and carted off to jail. Some onlooking people, staff persons and on-hand students as well, shook their heads in awe as Andy, wearing metal handcuffs, was driven away from the school. But quite a number of them, especially black students, cheered with joy. To them, it was a comeuppance well overdue.

Now, some people claimed that Andy was hit with a substantial lawsuit, but, personally, I was never sure of that. But there was one thing very certain. Reportedly, Andy had never, ever unleashed his aggression on any Caucasian student and, after his arrest on that fateful afternoon, he never, ever assaulted another African-American student either. To yours truly, that was a good thing.

Case No. 4 When I was a teen-aged high school student, I was visiting one of my close running buddies at his home one afternoon. It was a mild summer day, the sun was shining brightly and a slight breeze was blowing, so instead of sitting in the house, my friend, his mother and I decided to sit on the front porch, casually talking and joking on occasion.

My buddy's mother, who was forty-something and slightly

plump, was always pleasant to me and I liked her quite a lot also. In addition, she was somewhat dark-skinned (not that that feature bothered me - it didn't), but, apparently, it bothered my pal's mom to the max.

I, along with her son and daughter (who chose to stay in the house on the day I'm recounting), was well-aware of the mother's self-defacing feelings about herself, but, seemingly, the three of us (the non-adults) took it all in stride. We were used to hearing the lady of the house complain about being "black as the ace of spades (which she was not)" and begrudgingly saying she was "cursed at birth," all due to her disenchantment with the color of her skin. Almost traditionally, I dismissed her seriousness regarding the matter, and I hoped her endeared loved ones (like my buddy and his big sister) felt likewise.

However, on the particular day I'm recalling, when a very petite and very light-skinned African-American woman strolled up the adjacent walkway, obviously intent upon speaking to all or one of us, I found myself reassessing my former feelings.

Our unexpected visitor, who was toting a brown satchel, politely announced she was an 'Avon Products' representative and tried to entice my friend's mother to listen to her sales pitch. However, the discussion between the two females was short-lived at best, and was not at all productive. Therefore, minutes later, the saleslady bided us 'good day' and walked away, seemingly headed for a house that was located directly across the street from our vantage point.

Fortunately, the roving saleswoman was not within earshot when my friend's mom opted to almost begrudgingly reply. "God Almighty knows He ought to be ashamed of His self. Giving that homely looking' woman all that beautiful light colored skin. He could have given it to me, instead of wasting it all on that plain-Jane looking' heifer. Some people are just born in God's favor, I guess."

My buddy flashed his eyes almost hopelessly to the sky but I

"UP CLOSE AND PERSONAL"

elected to address his mother's verbal lament. "You've got beautiful skin, Mrs. Davis," I grimacingly replied. "Light, bright and damn near white" ain't so darn important. I think you're attractive, just the way you are. Don't put yourself down like that!"

"You can't tell my Mama nothing, Lonnie," my long-time pal tiredly spoke. "She wants to look like Lena Horne or Dorothy Dandridge or somebody."

"Not really," was Mrs. Davis's snap response to her son. "I just hate being stuck with this blue-black skin, that's all."

"But why, Mrs. Davis?" I injected. "I don't understand. First off, you're not that dark. They say, 'Clothes don't make the man.' So . . . skin color doesn't make the woman either."

"That's easy for you to say, Lonnie," the woman sadly responded. "You're a pretty tan color, not dark like me. And you're a handsome little boy too."

I guess I should have been appreciative of Mrs. Davis' compliment; instead, I was flustered and contrary. "But that's not that important either, Mrs. Davis," I argued. "Good looks are only skin deep. None of that is really important. My father's light-skinned and he's so full of himself, it's a crying shame! He even calls himself a 'pretty man.' But that doesn't make him a good father, or even a good man. He's mean and abusive. And you know what they say in the Bible, Mrs. Davis, don't you? 'Lucifer' - they say in the Bible that he was the most beautiful angel in God's kingdom. But as you know, he turned out to be the devil, Satan his self! My old man's like Lucifer."

At that juncture, even as I took a moment to calm myself after my rather emotional tirade, Mrs. Davis displayed a peculiar smile. "But, Lonnie," she stated, "I'd bet you a dollar for a donut that Lucifer has beautiful, light-colored skin."

Both, I and the woman's son guffawed at that point. And Mrs. Davis had to chuckle herself when I tiredly said, "Mrs. Davis, you are a real doozie. I don't know what we're going to do with you. You're absolutely hopeless!"

UP-CLOSE AND PERSONAL

Case No. 5 In June of 1962, I made a major change in my life. After graduating from high school on June 4th, I became a soldier in the United States Army on June the 20th. Without telling any of my high school running buddies about my pre-planned enlistment transition (and some of them graduated with me), I was administered the military oath and, in the company of approximately 40 other black young men whom I didn't know, we boarded a large bus that was headed to the distant Fort Leonard Wood, Missouri.

Of course, traditional 'basic training' awaited us at—that well-known military complex and we "*cruits*" (that's what our black Drill Instructor called us, saying that we had to work hard to earn the "r-e" that proceeded that term) well-knew it would not be like a 'Sunday picnic' or a 'walk in the park' and we were collectively right on the money about that.

The training that ensued was physically and mentally challenging, rigorous, exhausting, toilsome, grueling, unrelenting and any other descript term that required human resilience and fortitude. Speaking for myself, military basic training was everything (and more) that I had anticipated prior to reciting the oath of loyalty to the U.S. of A.

Subsequently, after going through something that was deemed 'zero week,' eight weeks of basic training immediately kicked in and we (meaning us cruits) were off to the races. However, to my utter joy, something rather bizarre occurred. Although I grieved over my boyhood chums when I left St. Louis, I was soon awarded an unexpected blessing. In less than two weeks' time, I had met, interacted and bonded with a fellow 18 year old Saint Louisan and, almost instantly, I felt endeared to him and him to me. And being an individual of heartfelt sentiment, I recognized him as my 'best friend' and I loved being around him. I called him 'Jay' and, to me, he was a bonafide godsend.

Therefore, in early August, when we had completed over half

"UP CLOSE AND PERSONAL"

of the basic training mechanism, we (meaning, the select group of men who originally boarded that army bus back on June 20th), were granted a 3-day, weekend pass and my newfound friend and I looked forward to returning to our mutual home-town, which, of course, was Saint Louis.

I'm certain it would surprise no one who ever knew me that movie-going played an endearing and cohesive role in my rapidly-formed, close-knit alliance with a young man whom I had known less than three months. And, so, when we took advantage of that 3-day pass, my buddy and I were intent upon seeing a first-run film while visiting Saint Louis.

We arrived in town around five o'clock in the evening on the first day of our pass. That was a Friday. We visited our respective families, then rendezvoused with a trio of my civilian high school chums (at an accommodating bar, of all places) and, there, Jay and I etched out plans to meet up and catch a movie on the next afternoon, Saturday.

Before leaving Leonard Wood, we had taken the initiative to ask our D.I. (Drill Instructor) if it was okay to wear fatigues (our standard duty uniforms) in the city and he casually answered affirmatively. So, when we elected to dress ourselves in fatigues for our movie outing, we were totally unaware of what was in store for us.

We were casually strolling down a renowned city avenue called 'Grand' and was headed for an equally renowned St. Louis movie theatre called the 'Fox.' It was a beautiful, mild summer afternoon and we were anxious to reach our intended destination.

However, when we were but a half a mile from the movie house, suddenly everything went horribly awry. When a military police squad car pulled over to the adjacent curb about fifteen yards in front of us, we immediately stopped our advance and watched as two sedate-faced M.P.'s disembarked the vehicle. One was black, the other one was white and although both of them were wearing private first class patches, the African-American soldier established himself as the leading spokesman. Both of them appeared to be in their early twenties.

"Where in the hell are you two Dumbo's going?" the black soldier angrily asked. "You got to know you're not authorized to wear fatigues in public! What's wrong with you two niggas?"

When I responded, my tone was just as gruff as the black M.P.'s was. "We're headed for the Fox theatre," I began. "And our Drill Instructor, back in Fort Leonard Wood, said it was alright to wear fatigues in the city."

"You're a goddamn lie!" shouted the African-American spokesman. "Little nigga, stop lying on your damn D.I.!"

Jay stood silently by, holding what was known as an officer's 'swagger stick,' but I wasn't at all speechless. "We don't have any reason to lie to you, man," I stated.

"Well, stop doin' it then!" yelled the angry-faced black spokesman as he opted to turn his attention to Jay. "Boy, where'd you get that fuckin' swagger stick?" he asked my friend.

"I bought it at the Post Exchange," Jay answered. However, the black questioner wasn't quite through. "And where did you get that hard fatigue hat you're wearing?" he asked, stepping towards Jay.

Again, my buddy's response was the Post Exchange. But, still, our African-American antagonist wasn't quite finished. "And where did you get that 'sharp-shooters' medal?" he quizzed, still picking on Jay.

Once again, my buddy cited the Post Exchange and that prompted the black PFC to grinningly say, "Aw, you're the goddamn P.X. (Post Exchange) kid, aren't you?"

At that precise juncture, the bystanding white M.P. decided to speak up for the very first time. He addressed his riding partner, suggesting, "Why don't we just let 'em go back home, and have 'em change clothes? Give them a warning."

"Naw, we're gonna lock up these two niggas," the black M.P. balked. "Teach 'em a lesson, one they'll never forget. Get the handcuffs."

Now, I didn't know if the two M.P.'s were in the midst of a 'good cop - bad cop' routine, but initially I couldn't believe they were serious in their ongoing actions. Seemingly sincere, the Caucasian M.P. made one more plea to his partner to let us off with a "warning," but it, too, fell on black indifferent and deaf ears. Alternately, we were handcuffed, placed in the backseat of the squad car and promptly driven to the military jail. There, we were permitted to call home, to apprise our respective mothers of our whereabouts and, subsequently, were locked up.

Then, the very next afternoon, which was Sunday, we were released and had just enough time to go to our individual homes, take a quick shower, don our khaki uniforms, eat a meal and make it to the site where the return bus awaited us. And by four P.M., as Jay and I sat together on that bus, we were en route back to Fort Leonard Wood, Missouri.

Owing to the mean-spirited and self-loathing antics of a young fellow African-American soldier, a 3-day, weekend pass was turned into an enduring and unredemptive nightmare. And to be grievously frank, presently, almost six decades later, I still cannot quite come to grips with the perverse and foreboding mind-set of that black military police officer. And I'm certain I never will.

Postscript –

Although it was not humanly possible to recoup or expunge the 24 hours that were cruelly stolen from my and Jay's lives by that self-hating M.P. (that yesteryear day was gone forever), an interesting footnote emerged almost three years later.

When I was officially discharged from the United States army on June 20th of 1965, I chose to take a Greyhound bus home rather than take a plane out at 'San Antonio International Airport.' However, I wasn't being thrifty or cheap, it was just that I always enjoyed riding across country (taking in the scenery and all) and it would grant me the opportunity to reminisce my military past and contemplate my forthcoming civilian life as well.

I was a sergeant E-5 by then and although I was actively recruited and encouraged to reenlist (by my Commanding Officer, the colonel at my workplace and several fellow sergeants too), I, alternately, nixed the idea. To my personal sorrow, the adverse memories greatly surpassed the good ones.

A day later, when my bus pulled into the Greyhound bus depot, which was located in downtown Saint Louis, I rose from my seat, just as my travelling companions did, and walked into the terminal to await the unloading of the stored luggage, which, to me, was my army duffel bag. And that's when I sighted him.

Standing about 30 paces from my position and garbed in his military police uniform (and, apparently, on duty), was the same stern-faced military policeman (the 'him' who I alluded to) who so coldly and doggedly insisted upon locking me and my friend, Jay, up in August of 1962.

Momentarily, I was poised to say something derogatory to my former nemesis, lash out at the man in my pent-up anger, but I gradually squelched that inclination. Not because I was remotely fearful or even due to my innate forgiving nature. Instead, it was in light of a single, sobering factor. Nearly three years had come and gone since that summer of '62 happening, but, currently (as if time had stood still), the soldier was sporting a single stripe on his shoulder.

I couldn't refrain from shaking my head in marked disbelief and wonder! I asked myself, "What kind of man would remain in the military service for 'umpteen' years and retain the rank of a neophyte private first class?" But, right away, the answer to my query, sorrowfully, came to me: "Only a brooding, self-loathing, wash-out loner who is void of human compassion and any semblance of empathy." And with that analogy, I slung my duffel bag to my left shoulder and promptly left the Greyhound terminal.

"ANATOMY OF AN ORANGE LEMON"

IN THE SHORT AFTERMATH OF that rather bizarre and unexpected happening at the Greyhound bus station (whether it was fate or purely coincidental, I didn't know), I found myself reflecting on it at great lengths. I wasn't particularly gloating or inwardly shouting *"yippie,"* but, admittedly, I did extract a measure of self-satisfaction from it.

In my personal assessment, I have always had a writer's mind and I'm quite analytical to boot, so I could not help from wondering about that black PFC's underlying story. Not only was I curious about his, seemingly, frozen rank status, I wanted to know what actually made him 'tick.' And if it was any way possible, without prejudice, I would have liked to have interviewed him.

Since that was the gist of my official job back at Fort Sam Houston, Texas (interviewing and conversing with hospitalized military personnel), then, maybe, that partly motivated me. But that wasn't all of it. I longed to take an in-depth look into the man's life (his past as well as his, then, present one) and, hopefully, arrive at a reasonable and viable consensus. The yesteryears actions he subjected Jay and myself to was not only unjust and overly harsh, it was simply illogical and evil-inspired.

Certainly, it wasn't lethal or even physically painful in the final analysis, but, to me (and, probably, Jay also), it was an example of "Man's inhumanity to man" on a relatively small-scale. And although I was fully aware that numerous white Americans were not strangers to such age-old brutality and mistreatment actions (especially when it came to people of color), I could not 'wrap my head around' a fellow black man behaving in such a comparable and gung-ho fashion.

Certainly also, in spite of the fact that Jay and I would have been just as stressed-out and angry had both M.P.'s been of the Caucasian persuasion, the mere realization that a so-called "brother" was the major vanguard behind our ensuing incarceration was ten-times more difficult to stomach. And in my opinion, that single factor greatly eclipsed the 'locking up' procedure itself.

In retrospect, those yesteryear dual-headed episodes (our 1962 incarceration and my rather weird 1965 scene at that bus terminal) were symbolic of my entire life. Unlike my dear friend, Jay, I had seen the inside of a jail cell as a teenager and I had already been exposed to my share of self-loathing blacks during the same time-frame. And as time marched forward, it was an uncanny prelude to what was to come.

Even as a pre-teen, I knew I'd have a tough row to hoe in life. In being a stickler for righteousness and justice (not 'just us'), as well as a staunch advocate for basic logic, I fully expected to, on occasion, lock horns with a select group of individuals who were contrary or diametrically opposed to my ideals.

As I stated before, none of us are perfect (not even me), but I've always strived to be a man of principle and integrity and that driving force still persists today, here in the year 2020.

Now, you may label me 'naive' or accuse me of formerly living in a made-up, fantasy world, but I once believed that there were countless men and women, and especially elected American politicians, who were endowed with the same commendable character qualities that I hold so dear. But, unfortunately, I was grossly in error.

With the gradual implementation and rise of the 'Trumplican' party, I underwent a sobering metamorphosis. It is extremely difficult (if not, impossible) to function in a principled and

"ANATOMY OF AN ORANGE LEMON"

upstanding manner if a person willingly remains silent in the midst of continuous graft and corruption. And when that same person chooses to actively collude and 'wallow' in that ongoing sphere of corruption, tragically, it is proof-positive that he or she was entirely void of principles and scruples in the first place. I can't emphasize it enough, people basically do not change throughout their lives. And, just like Maya Angelou so elegantly stated, "If a 'person' tells you who they are - then believe them."

Although I cannot refrain from laughing when television's 'Judge Judy' poses the question (and I'm paraphrasing here) "Do you know when a teenager (or child) is lying? Their mouth is moving," I still apprise every young person I happen to dialogue with that, in the wise words of Benjamin Franklin, "Honesty is the best policy." However, when I refocus on Donald Trump's steadfast political (and civilian) mouthpieces, which is a relevant progression, I can't avoid wondering what they endorse onto their individual kids and any other youngsters they're exposed to.

When I was working around teenagers (inside urban high schools and, later on, driving a school bus also), and was made to contend with hostile and disrespectful boys and girls alike, I often thought of the respective parents who were raising them. It wasn't always a truism that, "When you see the son (or daughter), then you see the father (or mother) also," but in many cases, that analogy holds steadfast water.

So, during the impeachment hearings, when it came to grown people (essentially Trumplicans) who actively stood in line to lie, misrepresent and stonewall on behalf of a despicable and unlawful POTUS like Donald John Trump, it became crystal clear to me why there are so many mixed-up and screwed-up children in America.

And I may sound like a broken record, but I still contend that an adult is waging a losing battle when they persistently tell a child to, "Do as I say," instead of "Do as I do." And angry and disgruntled people, and especially my Caucasian brothers and sisters, can cuss me and call me 'a sack of black niggas,' but I perceive my analogy as, "The truth crushed to earth." (Alternately, "It will rise again."). Therefore, name-calling cannot alter or diminish it.

However, who knows what the future holds for Trump loyalist? All children aren't dumb, gullible or spineless. Maybe, a select few of them will, one day, muster up the nerve or courage to verbally take exception to their parent's hypocrisy and poor example.

I imagine that Trumplican congressmen and senators may explain away their prevaricating and stonewalling positions by referencing their desire for reelection or their overt lust for wealth and power, but it's superficial at best. Then, again, maybe their kids don't care one way or the other, maybe they're indifferent or entirely ignorant of their parent's ongoing behavior and maybe, too, the respective offsprings are perennial "chips off the old block."

And, in that case, the applicable parents have nothing to be concerned about. As long as the parents can continue to put food on the table, shelter them and sate their kid's material desires, the parents are probably joyous in their established comfort zone.

But there's one truism about 'lying' and remaining loyal to those misconceptions and distortions, and it is, "One lie always prompts, yet, a follow-up lie or two." Therefore, if a child of a Trump surrogate someday askes their father or mother to explain and justify Donald Trump's maniacal thirst for vengeance and relentless punishment for anyone who dares to oppose or defy him, then, as that parent, be ready to add one more lie to an already-overflowing falsified playbook.

I just hope the subject parent will be spontaneous and somewhat creative in their response. Personally, I have always viewed Trump as a petty, thin-skinned, vindictive and self-absorbed bully but, of course, I'm biased when it comes to the man.

Hopefully, the focal parent will not cite him as a "counterpuncher." That's a patented and worn-out cliché and is a precise synonym for the 'bully' I know Trump to be. Maybe, the Trumplican parent could liken the POTUS to Michael Corleon in 'Godfather - Part 2.' If you recollect that movie, Michael, as the Godfather, was hell-bent on 'wiping out' all of his enemies. Of course, I'm just trying to be helpful.

Of course, too, I was only joking and being subtlety facetious. Trumplican politicians and die-hards who march lock-step with their immature and arrogant leader do not need any advice about being 'inventive' and 'disingenuous.' During the past three years or so, they have become expert and polished regarding those two evasive traits.

However, there is nothing that remotely predicates or justifies the President's unprecedented craving for vengeance and pay back. No matter how an onlooker slices or dices it when it comes to the President's post-impeachment conduct, a mountain of evidence and sworn testimony proved he was guilty of the charges levelled on him. Republican stonewalling prevented him from being removed from office, but no degree of after-the-fact retribution, no matter how harsh, could wipe Trump's conviction status from the slate.

This is the outstanding 'kicker' in the matter, however; a prominent aspect that greatly supersedes Donald Trump's well-publicized vendetta itself. In spite of the vast majority of the Republican Party, in their hearts, they well-knew that our Chief Executive was guilty as charged when it came to the Ukraine scandal.

In addition, the majority of them were cognizant of the fact that the nonpartisan witnesses who were called to testify during the impeachment hearings were telling the truth. Apparently, they didn't care about that factor either. And if I was afforded the opportunity to address each of them individually, there's a single question I would pose to every one of them. And that query would be, "Is there absolutely no limit to your hypocrisy?"

Naturally, I would not hold my breath, awaiting a credible response to my question. Instead, I would consider the source, fully knowing that even the sky itself was not a feasible limit. In actuality, that group's embedded allegiance to Donald Trump has no measurable bounds either. And that explains why they collectively stood by silent and idle when the POTUS implemented his vendetta assault. Although they knew those targeted former witnesses were doing their civic duty when they appeared at those fact-finding hearings, seemingly, none of them were opposed to Trump's persecutory behavior in the aftermath of those congressional proceedings. But even worse, many of those Republican loyalist enthusiastically and, without conscience, joined Trump's begrudging caravan.

Upon being perfectly candid, I don't know what to say about Donald Trump's pro-partisan allies or his fanatical base either. They are a collective enigma wrapped inside an impenetrable enigma. Whether they are evil-incarnated, completely brainwashed, barren of basic scruples and morals or in search of a tangible god or savior, I can't quite size them up.

But Donald John Trump, the man, is by no means a mystery to me. I seriously believe he has been true-to-form throughout his privileged and rather warped life. Being a born sociopath and narcissist and enamored with great wealth and the unharnessed power it wields, he was the infamous "spoiled brat" and, owing to numerous close-knit lackeys who are in awe of his riches (and, at present, his presidential position as well), he's a "spoiled" and self-grandiose elderly man.

Throughout Trump's almost storybook life, he has undeservingly been exalted. He's been catered to, cowered down to, showered with unearned praise and accolades and continually told he is substantially better and superior to the greater majority of the people who populate the world, and especially minorities. And that's why, in spite of doggedly concealing his scholastic history from the public, he perceives himself as an expert on every and anything.

However, in addition to all of Trump's aforementioned flaws, foibles and idiosyncrasies, I believe he shares a commonality with an inordinate number of people (especially youthful ones) whom I've known during my lifetime. The POTUS not only hates being told "NO," he takes it personal and, habitually, resorts to retribution and punishment directly aimed at the naysayer. And it is singularly because, like an immature child, he firmly believes, "If you are not solidly for me, then you are against me."

When it comes to the world of friendship, many young people (too many of them, in fact) operate within the premise that, "If you are truly my friend, then I expect you to take my back (or side) and sanction any and every action I choose to take" (and regardless if it's right or wrong).

Personally speaking, I have always encouraged youngsters to draw a line at the 'right or wrong' juncture. I convey to them, also, that if your heart tells you that an action is essentially wrong, then step away and walk in the opposite direction of it. And who knows? Maybe, your friend will have second thoughts about the issue also. In life, friendships come and go (and especially fair weather ones), but integrity and principles should not be easily compromised and not even in the name of friendship.

Sorrowfully, Donald Trump takes loyalty and devotion to a different level, and, oftentimes, a nefarious level. He fully expects and demands that all people (whether they are Republicans or not) take him at his word and, heaven forbid, challenge his veracity. To be clear, solely because he occupies the office of the Presidency of the United States, Trump thoroughly expects every American (not 'some' or even 'most') to accept, without question, his lies and exaggerations as the gospel truth.

And although that thought-pattern is eerily reminiscent of a former disgraced and desposed Republican president named Richard M. Nixon, the entire Republican Party (save Mitt Romney) bought into the dictatorial nonsense. In my estimation, it distinctly defines and typifies the surging 'Trumplican Party.'

Throughout Donald Trump's rather unsavory existence, his entire life has been about his inflated ego, his inherited wealth and his presumed white superiority. With the exception of his immediate family, he doesn't sincerely care about the well-being or plight of 'any' human being and sees them as minor pawns and mere stepping stones to aid him in achieving his personal goals.

Being sociopathic by nature, Trump deems himself superior and elitist and truly feels that he is not only above the law and totally exempt from all rules and regulations, he, alone, is vested with the power and authority to interpret and sanction any and every orthodox guideline in existence. In essence, "right" and "wrong" is subject to his, seemingly, 'royal' discretion and whims.

Therefore, operating under the guise of his own, self-composed manifesto, Trump has always done anything and everything he deems necessary to secure and promote his ambitions and agenda. And, tragically, that pertains to his past, his present and his future also.

Whether you (the reader) are pro-Trump or con-Trump, unless you were comatose or mentally challenged at the time, you cannot convince me (or anyone else) that you sanctioned or remotely understood the would-be President's hypocrisy when he proudly assembled and showcased a group of women who accused "former" President Bill Clinton of adultery and a myriad of sexual improprieties.

Although William Jefferson Clinton was not opposing him for the presidency, Trump callously saw it as fair game and appropriate to, in some nefarious way, taunt and taint Hillary Clinton by highlighting her husband's past indiscretions. Personally, since it was common knowledge that Donald Trump, himself, has always been a notorious philanderer and a consorter of prostitutes and porn stars as well, I equated it with insanity!

In the short aftermath of that cruel-hearted and ugly televised maneuver, I asked myself (and I'd like to pose the same query to Trump's steadfast base also) - "What kind of person, who has a history of immersing himself in the same murky waters, finds comfort in exposing and chiding another individual for the exact

"ANATOMY OF AN ORANGE LEMON"

indiscretion or sin?" (People who live in glass houses should not throw stones.).

And although I'll never know the answer, I always wondered what Melania Trump thought of her husband's tactic also. Did she approve of it? Evidently, she did. Otherwise, in good faith, how on earth could she choose to champion an 'Anti-Bullying' cause? Or, was it in line with the "Birds of a feather" philosophy?

However, when I reverted back to my question about Donald Trump. When I wondered about his audacious and hypercritic behavior when it came to that assembled parade of Bill Clinton haters, the answer practically jumped out at me. What kind of man would stoop to such a mean-spirited and low life tactic?

Specifically, a man who feels he's elite and entitled, and sincerely believes he's above the law and exempt of all rules and regulations and, therefore, is rendered unaccountable for any semblance of wrongdoing or missteps. And that distinctly defines President Donald John Trump.

Throughout my life, I've heard people say, "If you give some people an inch, they will take a mile. So, when it came to 2019's 'Hunter Biden - Ukraine' issue, I instantly revisited my summation on Trump's unorthodox tactics when he was still on the campaign trail.

Although he 'boldly' placed his daughter, Ivanka, and her husband, Jared Kushner, on the White House payroll, he thought nothing of 'boldly' charging former Vice-President Joe Biden of nepotism when it came to Biden's only remaining son, Hunter, and specifically linking it to Ukraine corruption as well.

However, when it was later disclosed that Trump was using a four hundred million dollar aid package as a bargaining chip (which alleged that the POTUS was secretly coercing Ukraine's President Zelensky to announce that Hunter Biden was under investigation), Trump quickly backed off, claiming there was no "Quid Pro Quo." Essentially, that meant there was no such deal in the offing. In the aftermath (when the heat was on), the President announced he would "never" ask a foreign country to aid him politically (especially when it came to the election process), but, conveniently, he forgot he had emphatically implored Russia to, "Find Hillary Clinton's missing E-mails" when he was on the campaign trail. That, too, is called hypocrisy.

But Trump's surrogates, especially the ones in the U.S. Senate, didn't believe any of the charges levelled against the POTUS. They chose, instead, to believe that the Ukraine president was naive. That, somehow, he was unaware or unconcerned with the impending aid package (which, by the way, was held up from July to September) and were delighted to hear the Ukrainian leader say there was no extortion (or 'Quid Pro Quo') involved.

But I must ask you: In the event that the country of Ukraine might seek further monetary aid from America in the future, what could or should he have said? (Under the same circumstances, what would you have said?). The crying shame of it all was that the country of Ukraine was already trying to cast-off a blanket of internal graft and corruption when it's relatively new leader was practically strong-armed (by the American POTUS) and was obliged to crawl right back under it. My empathetic heart went out to President Zelensky and the entire populace of that struggling country.

Naturally though, my irrepressible empathy did not distinguish after the Ukraine scandal or after Donald Trump's impeachment trial either. In fact, it reached full throttle when the President actively launched his shameful vengeance rampage.

And it especially affected me because, firstly, whether I was in the military or civilian life, I habitually strived for excellence in job performance, secondly, I frequently engaged in endearing and close-knit relationships with my fellow co-workers at my varied places of employment and, thirdly, I've always been adamant (if not, dogmatic) about being honest and upstanding regarding every matter, and even in the face of repercussions.

Therefore, when Donald John Trump, a man who never applied

or searched for a real job in his entire privileged life, an individual who is completely foreign to true friendship or comradeship and an aspiring demigod who is, undoubtedly, ethically-challenged, came forth and boisterously publicized his post-impeachment vendetta, I wasn't surprised in the least regarding the President's begrudging behavior. Mimicking the words of many of the man's supporters, "It was Trump just being Trump."

Admittedly, there was one aspect of the impeachment proceedings and its aftermath that did take me, somewhat, aback. Throughout Trump's presidency, various T.V. 'talking heads' often longed for the POTUS to "act presidential." I always branded it 'wishful thinking,' but when I caught Trump on the television in the midst of his blood-thirsty crusade to punish his impeachment hearing enemies, he proved he did have a few acting skills.

Speaking into the camera with a stern, straightforward face, he portrayed the anonymous whistle blower as the traitorous 'Benedict Arnold' and went on to make hearing witnesses such as William Taylor, Maria Yovanavich, Gordon Sondland and Lt. Col. Vindman akin to Julius and Ethel Rosenberg, the couple who were executed as American spies in the 1950's. And he spoke with so much sincerity and so much conviction that I emerged convinced that he honestly saw merit in his distorted viewpoints and earnestly believed he was right also!

And that's why I perceive him as dangerous (to our country and himself as well) and certifiably insane too!

Now, before I close out this book, I feel compelled to tell you (my book's readers) why I elected to label my final chapter, "Anatomy of an Orange Lemon." However, a person would not have to be Sherlock Holmes or Columbo to partially deduce its meaning.

Goes without saying, I strongly dislike President Donald John Trump and, as evidenced by this book, I make no bones about my feelings. I deem him a "lemon," plainly because I consider him a self-serving washout as a human being and I branded him "orange" solely due to his skin color on my television set. Neither of those hue descriptions have anything to do, whatsoever, with racial identity. However, it does afford me an opportunity to pay homage to a well-known Reverend Dr. Martin Luther King Jr. quote.

When Dr. King delivered his 'I Have a Dream' speech way back in 1963, he encouraged America not to "judge black people by the color of their skin, but by the content of their character."

Therefore, I submit to you that, throughout this book, I wasn't judging Donald Trump by the color of his skin, but by the content of his character. The verdict is now in the hands of the jury.

★ **THE END** ★

EPILOGUE

"What the world needs now, is love, sweet love,
it's the only thing that there's just too little of."

THE ABOVE LYRICS WERE SUNG by a yesteryear singer named Jackie DeShannon, among others, and it has always been one of my favorite tunes. The words were unarguably true 'way back when' and they especially resonate today, here in 2020 in the throes of a devastating pandemic plaguing our nation.

Literally thousands and thousands of people in the world have contracted that relentless virus and tens of thousands of those people are seriously ill and/are hospitalized in the wake of it. And, more grievously, the staggering death toll escalates by the day, if not by the hour.

Evidently, unlike millions of people in this world (and especially in America), the disease is indiscriminate and directly contrary to America's current President, is totally unbiased and oblivious to territorial boundaries and limits as well. In essence, the epidemic is an equal-opportunity disease that's obviously unimpressed by a person's race, religion, wealth, fame or station in life and is distinctly international in scope and aggression.

Of course, every facet of the foregoing commentary is tragic, alarming and mournful as well. Currently, at the end of March 2020, the pandemic is all over the map, nations are practically barraged with it on television, radio and every other media outlet in existence and the entire known world is in a collective and

EPILOGUE

unmitigated tizzy. Mental dread, anxiety and fear of the unknown is commonplace throughout the world.

Admittedly, I, too, worry, so I'm not above the fray either. However, I, as a compassionate American, was fretful and deeply worried well-before that pandemic prevailed in any region of the world. I was greatly concerned and saddened by our country's state of turmoil, hatred and indifference.

In the wake of all the inner city crime and violence, the various school shootings and random massacres, the increase in youth suicides and the marked upsurge in racial and anti-Semitic animus, how should I have felt? And, in addition, when an unlawful American President (Donald Trump, of course) is allowed to almost, magically, transform "wrong" into "right" and have his political minions sanction and openly endorse his illusion, how should any person who loves justice and fair play feel?

While there's no getting around the fact that the current pandemic is the worst thing that has happened to the American province in modern time (it even eclipses the attack on Pearl Harbor and 911 itself), I pray and hope it will, somehow, be a game-changer.

Of course, I find no delight in seeing human suffering and heartfelt sorrow. My heart goes out to the thousands of people who, subsequently, mourn lost loved ones and I genuinely lament the deceased victims as well. I even silently dislike the imposed 'distancing premise,' a mechanism that directs people to refrain from being intimate and physically touching others. And, personally, it has nothing to do with any semblance of sexual conduct. I've always been somewhat of a serial 'hugger' and that's an action I truly miss.

But, in quite a few ways, the virus has already had a significant impact on America in general. Whether people agree or not, it highlighted Donald Trump's innate ineptness and dispassion in handling a catastrophic and enduring crisis. Certainly, he could

UP-CLOSE AND PERSONAL

not be blamed for implementing it or for not seeing it on the horizon either.

However, it did force Trump to take a step back and surrender to science and prevent him from foolishly announcing, "I know more than the scientist know." Who knows? Maybe, one day he'll rethink his long-time denial of 'climate change.' Naturally, I won't hold my breath in hopes of it.

Also, when I focus on the average American citizen, and think specifically about how the pandemic proceeded to cripple and all-but destroy our country's economy, I can't refrain from wondering about the previous mind-set of those fellow Americans when it came to foreign country of Ukraine.

I imagined that many of them, not all of them, wholeheartedly bought into the rationalized commentary that was echoed by Trump loyalist after the aid package was finally released. Although the POTUS was roundly criticized for putting the brakes on the Ukraine assistance package from July to September 2019 (over 60 days), a select group of 'Trumplicans' (as well as many of his base) casually claimed it was "no big deal" and, essentially, said the stall was a minor, virtually irrelevant inconvenience.

But in early March of 2020, when everyday people started losing or were laid off of jobs in droves and when money sources began to dry up and dissipate entirely (all because of the pandemic), I wondered if their minds recalled the Ukraine fiasco. Specifically, if they were amongst the 'rationalizers' I alluded to, could they, themselves, adjust to a prolonged drought in monetary assistance?

Like I asked in an early chapter in this book, "If those cavalier individuals (meaning, lockstep Trump loyalist) were made to live from payday to payday, would a lengthy delay in personal monetary wages or funds be problematic to them?"

Notably, the Trump surrogates on Capitol Hill (all of them, Republicans) were not subject to a stoppage of a single pay check, but that did not apply to the average American Joe or JoAnne. Unfortunately, many of the latter were (and are still) in a monetary

EPILOGUE

quandary in the wake of the 2020 plague, which is similar to the foreign country of Ukraine back in July and August of 2019. It's something to think about.

Throughout this book, I frequently talked about my irrepressible optimism and idealism and even in the presence of a horrific and dreadful scourge like the current one, I still have residual hope for a stellar and bright future. And, ironically (although it's difficult to fathom), certain aspects of the scourge itself heightens my hope and optimism.

Grievously, absolutely nothing can restore life to the multitude of precious loved ones who have succumbed to the plague thus far. And, inevitably, scores of other people will be subjected to the same terminal fate. In addition, hundreds of thousands of people throughout the world will be stricken by the virus and will, prayerfully, survive it as well.

Most certainly, it is all so tragic, so heartbreaking, so unfathomable and so indescribably awful too, but even in the dark of our nation's most grievous hour, I see a silver lining. This horrific scourge will gradually dissipate and, eventually, will vanish altogether, but even in the midst of our deepest mourning and long-enduring lament, the peoples of the world, regardless of the respective locales, will recover from the devastation and, hopefully, will go forth with a brand new agenda and a novel sense of purpose.

According to biblical scriptures, "The love (actually 'lust') of money is the root of all evil" and although I cannot justly speak for other nations, I know that verse is astutely true of America. As I stated in, yet, another chapter in this book, 'money' and 'power' ruled the roost in our nation and God was frequently placed on the back burner (that is, if He was anywhere on the stove at all).

Therefore, prior to the deadly plague, that was the driving force behind the collective heart of most Americans. Even if a modest alteration comes forth after the virus pronouncedly subsides or vanishes, I would likely view it as a vast improvement from pre-plague days.

UP-CLOSE AND PERSONAL

Although countless individuals will chide and decry my optimism altogether, as well as label my personal aspirations as 'wishful thinking,' I deem my feelings as markedly feasible and logical.

Call it conjecture, but prior to the onset of the epidemic, the average American citizen was almost explicitly fixated on themselves and their immediate families. Currently (and for many days and weeks to come), as the virus literally ravages the entire world, those "average American citizens" are persuaded, if not compelled to emerge from their self-constructed cocoon and take heed of the dire plight and suffering of others, even people who exist out-side their family circle.

Essentially, that is where we are at this juncture in modern America. Hopefully, in post-pandemic times (and I pray for the dawning of those days), we, as a country, will finally realize that we are intricately connected and spiritually linked and are, indeed, our "brother's keeper."

Of course, my aspirations are rather idealistic and bathed in faith also. However, even staunch non-believers will one day be compelled to cite the 2020 pandemic as a game-changer also.

At present, even if unbelievers emerge personally unscathed by the effect of the national monetary crisis, unless they are cold and unduly heartless, they are resigned to aiding and assisting loved ones who are struggling and suffering from it.

In addition, those same faith-resistant people will be made to deal with catastrophic sickness and the entity of death also. In stark reality, they, themselves, and anyone and everyone around them are susceptible to the scourge and could very well succumb to it as well. Sorrowfully, there is no safe haven for any man, woman or child who walks the earth.

However, my inner feelings about the effect of the plague is more focused on the living instead of the deceased and I'll address it now. Throughout this book I spoke of being a sensitive and sentimental man. In addition, I often confessed to being a movie-going fanatic as well. And when I mix those particular traits, I admit to, sometimes, shedding tears when watching sad films too. As I've said before, I am not ashamed of those feelings either.

Therefore, when I reference a yesteryear movie called "*The Roy Campanella Story*" as a focal point, no reader should be remotely surprised by it. It was based on real life and was about a popular Negro baseball catcher (Campanella) who played for the old 'Brooklyn Dodgers.' Due to a horrific automobile accident, Mr. Campanella was paralyzed from the shoulders on down. And that, for a prolonged period of time, included his arms and legs.

The foregoing was unimaginably tragic and heartrending in itself. But compounding Mr. Campanella's mental pain and misery was the fact that he had a troubled and very distraught young son. To be perfectly honest, although I watched that film in its entirety, my memory of it is rather vague at present. But one scene made an indelible mark on my heart and brain.

Roy Campanella, while sitting in his wheelchair, was looking up at his anguish-filled and weeping son, and upon surrendering to his own tears, softly said, "My arms ache to hold you." And when I heard that poignant declaration, I, too, was bawling. For I deeply felt Mr. Campanella's sincerity.

Now, some readers may be asking, "What the hell does any of that have to do with the pandemic or the current state of affairs in America?" And I'll address that question to the best of my ability.

In the wake of the deadly virus, Americans and the people of other nations have been strongly advised to keep their physical distance from others, and regardless of the intimacy of the relationship. Furthermore, when a person is stricken with the disease and is, subsequently, hospitalized, loved ones are encouraged to keep their distance from the patient, and no matter how grave or terminal the pertinent patient's condition is.

In reality, those set guidelines are highly necessary and appropriate also but I anticipate and look forward to the day they will be safely relaxed and, eventually, banished altogether. But when they are, I am hopeful that my American countrymen and women will be resigned to the task of superseding our former distancing and estrangement with a renewed spirit of brotherly love and sincere affection. And I also pray that it will be highlighted and topped off with a firm and robust embracement. To me, it will be a day that's long-overdue and one that I have always relished and dreamed of.

In Jackie DeShannon's yesteryear song, she proclaimed "What the world needs now, is love, sweet love." And that, too, is long-overdue. And then, later on, John Lennon released a similar inspirational song called 'Imagine.' In it, he remarked "You may say I'm a dreamer, but I'm not the only one." And that's a comment I personally ascribe to. In my innate optimism, I truly believe there are others who share and cherish those same sentiments and aspirations. Hopefully, you, the reader, are one of them.

www.ingramcontent.com/pod-product-compliance
Lightning Source LLC
LaVergne TN
LVHW011944070526
838202LV00054B/4795